APOLLO'S CREED

APOLLO'S CREED

LESSONS I LEARNED from **MY ASTRONAUT DAD** RICHARD F. GORDON, JR.

TRACI SHOBLOM

Published 2023 by Gildan Media LLC
aka G&D Media
www.GandDmedia.com

Front cover design by Tom McKeveny

Interior design by Meghan Day Healey of Story Horse, LLC.

Library of Congress Cataloging-in-Publication Data is available upon request

ISBN: 978-1-7225-0640-7

10 9 8 7 6 5 4 3 2 1

To Carleen, Rick, Larry, Tom,
Jimmy, Diane, and Chris.

We are the keepers of the legacy.

Contents

A Message from the Author

"Shoot for the moon.
Even if you miss, you'll land among the stars."
—Norman Vincent Peale

Apollo's Creed is not a typical memoir, nor is it a typical self-help book. It's a hybrid. I've attempted to blend public facts about the space program and what happened before we met Richard with stories and anecdotes from our time together. But my years as a personal development writer have seeped into my DNA, and so I couldn't write a book that doesn't have practical application. To help you apply the content to your own life, you can visit the website AstronautDad.com and download a free workbook to help you engage with the life lessons. I encourage you to take these lessons and make them your own. Even though you may not have had an "astronaut dad," you can take the wisdom and use it to fuel your own success.

In this book, I've shared my personal stories, and some of the meaningful things Richard said to me in my thirty-nine years as his daughter. As much as this is my story, it's also yours. Take the messages and lessons and make them your own. And when you're done, I hope that you, too, can shoot for the moon and land among the stars.

Introduction

I got the call from my brother Chris at 6:30 in the morning on November 7, 2017. Chris is a cop and isn't the kind of guy who just calls to chat at that time of day, so I knew this wasn't a social call.

"What's up?" I asked, sleepily, knowing the answer as I asked the question.

"Hey, sis. I have bad news." He was calling to tell me that our stepfather had passed away late the night before.

To the world, he was Captain Richard F. Gordon Jr., Gemini and Apollo astronaut, Navy test pilot and winner of the Bendix Trophy, recipient of two Distinguished Flying Crosses, breaker of the transcontinental speed record. He'd received medals and honors and met presidents and dined with celebrities and dignitaries.

But, to me, he was "the Bear." He was the guy who married my mother when I was a rebellious teenager with a bad attitude toward authority. He was the guy I fought with, cried to, and celebrated with. The guy who told me to clean my room, take off my shoes before I came in the house, and said, "A job worth doing is worth doing right the first time." The astronaut? More like "Ass" tronaut, I'd mutter under my breath. He'd just look at me and smile at my stubborn antics and say, "I love you, Racy. You are your mother's daughter, that's for sure."

We always had a special connection; one that was different from the ones he had with his biological children or with even my brother Chris. I was his "baby girl." He called me "Racy" and I gave him the nickname "Bear" because of his tough exterior and his cuddly personality.

While my stepsiblings were the ones who watched their dad fly off into space, I was the one who'd benefited from the lessons that those experiences taught him. My stepsiblings had the guy who was still trying to "make it to the moon." I got the one who'd been there, done that, and got paid to tell the stories.

Living with him during my formative years shaped me into the person I am today. From him, I learned key life lessons on how to rise to the top of your field, how to be a person of integrity and loyalty, and how important it is to keep your sense of humor. Anyone who knew Dick Gordon knew how much fun he was.

Everyone can Google his name and see cool footage of the launches and the interviews. They can read how the rocket was struck by lightning during the launch of Apollo 12. You can watch the documentaries, see the interviews of the people who played Richard in movies. I still read and watch those things and learn something new about him almost every time I do. Space stuff is fun. But that's not what *Apollo's Creed* is about.

If you ask any of my siblings, they'd each give you different perspectives and different accounts of what he was like. After all, when you raise eight kids in sixteen years, you're going to get some different stories. His oldest daughter, Carleen, was fifteen when he went to the moon. I was fifteen when he married my mother. At his funeral, we all sat around and commented on how different each of our experiences with him was.

Apollo's Creed is my own personal story of being his daughter for thirty-nine years. It is about the private guy and the things he would say when the cameras were off. In it, I share the candid answers to the questions everyone always asks. It's filled with the at-home anecdotes that most people weren't around to see. When you've sat upon a rocket and set it on fire, been shot into outer space and then have been all alone in a space capsule, you get a different perspective on life. That's what *Apollo's Creed* is about. These are my stories—the funny ones, the profound ones, and the rare chance for a daughter to ask her dad, "So what was it like to go to the moon?"

What would he have thought about me writing this book? He'd have loved it. By being in the position to see some things that only a few human beings on the planet have ever seen, Richard gained a tremendous amount of wisdom, life experience, and, yes, perspective. He'd often said that if he hadn't become an astronaut, he probably would have become a teacher. I know that he would be thrilled to have his life lessons penned in a way that could teach readers like you and inspire them to live their best life. After all, that's what being his daughter did for me.

1.

There's Always Someone Better Than You

Don't Compare Yourself to Anyone Else

"Traci, can we eat the dessert first even though Mom is with us?" My eight-year-old brother, Chris, whispered this to me as he was sitting next to me on an airplane, in the window seat. His big brown eyes were fixated on the tray table before him and the airplane food that used to be served to every passenger on a cross-country flight. Our parents had been divorced for years, and we'd gotten used to traveling alone, and even though I was only twelve, he looked to me as a mother figure. It was our fun treat to eat the dessert first when we flew back and forth between our parents' homes in Miami, Florida, (Mom) and Lake Havasu City, Arizona (Dad).

Our mom was in the aisle seat, reading a magazine. Linda Saunders had the kind of striking beauty that made men turn their heads. She'd been a model, a radio and television personality, and her strawberry blonde hair, huge blue eyes, and dimpled, wide smile captured the attention of pretty much everyone in every room she walked into. My mother had "it" and knew it.

"Go ahead," I whispered to my brother. "By the time she notices it, your dessert will be gone!" He broke out into a gap-toothed grin and dug into the little piece of cake with the Christmas tree frosting on top of it.

The date was December 17, 1978, and my mom, brother, and I were flying from Miami to Las Vegas. She was going to go skiing with some friends, and Chris and I were going to see our dad and stepmom for Christmas. I didn't know it at the time, but the events that happened on that plane would change the trajectory of my life. That's why the date stuck in my head so clearly.

"Excuse me, ma'am?" The stewardess (as flight attendants were called back then) leaned over and spoke to my mother. "There is a gentleman at the back of the plane who would like to buy you a drink. Can I get you a glass of wine or something?"

She craned her head back, and I got on my knees to peer over the seat and see who we were talking about. There, in a seat that was several rows back, was a man with a head of dark brown hair, long sideburns, and a huge smile. He was holding up a plastic glass, as if it were a toast.

"Traci, give me a piece of paper and one of Chris's crayons," Mom said. She scribbled a note and handed it to the flight attendant. "Give him this and tell him thank you."

Sipping the champagne, she kept stealing looks back to see his reaction to her note. We heard a loud guffaw, and then a few moments later, the flight attendant returned, with a note. "He said to give you this."

Her face broke out into a huge smile as she read the note (keeping it away from my young eyes), she laughed, and then said to me, "I'll be right back. I'm going to go talk to him."

She moved back to the empty seat next to him and sat there for the rest of the flight. I never knew what he said in that note, but whatever it was sparked a thirty-nine-year romance that lasted until he died at eighty-eight years old.

In looking back, I realized that what happened on that plane was very "on brand" for him. He was a man who knew what he wanted and knew how to get it. Whether it was getting a beautiful woman into the seat next to him, or getting himself a seat on a rocket ship, Richard F. Gordon Jr. knew a thing or two about success. And, whether I liked it or not, I was going to learn some things about it too.

"Stop looking out the window, Traci. He's either going to come or he isn't. Go back out and talk with your friends." My mom was in the kitchen of our Miami house making snacks for my birthday party.

"No running by the pool!" she yelled, for the thousandth time.

It was the eve of my thirteenth birthday. All of my best friends and classmates had come for a pool party. Despite my mother's admonition, I couldn't keep my eyes off the front door. I'd invited my crush, David Crisp, and the only thing in the world I wanted for my birthday was for him to come to my party. He'd been walking me home from school for a few months, and we'd even progressed as far as holding hands. We talked on the phone every night and sat together at lunch. It felt like true love!

"Who's that guy with your mom?" My best friends Wendy Levine, Francie Bianco, and Karen Consolo and I were in the deep end of the pool, trying to stay away from my annoying little brother.

"Oh, that's Richard. My mom's boyfriend. He used to be an astronaut or something."

"No way."

"Way.

"I don't believe you. Did he go to the moon?"

"Yeah. I think it was the second mission or something. I don't really care. I'm just glad that he's distracting my mom from bugging me about my room and homework."

The doorbell rang and I practically levitated out of the pool. Was it David? My face must have visibly fallen when I saw that it was just the pizza guy, because Richard called me over to the table where he was sitting.

"Are you having fun at your party, Traci?"

"Yeah, I am."

"I noticed that you seem to be watching the door. Are you expecting someone special?"

I didn't really want to talk about this with him but didn't see that I had a choice. "Kind of."

"Is it a boy?" He looked at me with kind, hazel eyes. "It's a boy."

Just then, my mom came and set the pizza boxes down on the food table. She looked stunning in a white bikini with a floor length pink flowered sheer cover-up.

"He probably won't come anyway." I looked down at my feet, feeling fat and ugly in my green one-piece swimsuit. "I'm not pretty like my mom."

Richard took my chin and moved my head up so we were eye-to-eye. "Listen, Traci. I was a Navy test pilot and had to compete with some of the best pilots on the planet to decide who was going to get to go to NASA. Then, when we were in Gemini and Apollo training, we were all trained together. They didn't choose who was going to go to the moon until we were all trained. Do you know what I learned from that kind of intense competition?"

I shook my head.

"I learned that there's always going to be someone better than you. There's someone smarter, faster, stronger, taller, better lookin' than you. It's not about competing with anyone else. It's about competing with yourself to be the best YOU can be."

"But she's so beautiful. I can never be that beautiful." My eyes filled with tears as I watched my friends flock around her.

"She sure is beautiful. And if I told you that you are just as pretty as her, you wouldn't believe me anyway. So, I'll leave you with this and then I'm gonna go get some pizza before your brother and his friends get it all. You will never be Linda, Traci. Don't even try. You just be YOU, and trust me, you're pretty damn amazing."

If only I could have learned that lesson then.

2.

Houston? I Have a Problem

Do It Right the First Time

"Traci, Chris—can you come in here?" It was shortly after my birthday party, and my mom was sitting on the couch in the living room of our Miami house. We'd lived there only a few years, as Mom was coming out of a divorce from the man she married right after my father. She was working as a news writer and broadcaster for WINZ and had been offered a television job. I assumed that she was calling us together to talk about her new hours at work and wanted me to help out with Chris after school. I couldn't have been more wrong.

"I want to talk to you both about something."

We looked at her expectantly, but there was something familiar about the glow she had. This wasn't about work. It was about her boyfriend.

"You know that Richard and I have been seeing each other for a while, right?"

We nodded, and my heart sank. I knew where this was going. He was going to be moving in with us.

"Well, his job is in Texas, and it's really hard to have to fly back and forth. So—"

Here we go, I thought. We were going to have to share our new house with some guy my mom was dating.

"We're moving to Houston."

What?

"WHAT?" Tears sprang to my eyes. I had just gotten settled in Miami after the divorce. I didn't even want to move to Florida in the first place, but we did, and I finally made friends and had a boyfriend and everything. She'd married one guy I couldn't stand and that only lasted a year. Now she was moving us to Texas to follow some other guy?

"No. I'm not going."

"Can I bring my toys and the other stuff from my room?" Chris asked, with the innocence of a nine-year-old.

"Absolutely. We're bringing everything."

He was satisfied with that answer and ran off to his room, leaving me hurt and angry. "So, you're just going to leave your new job and our new house and what? Move us to the middle of nowhere, for what? Some guy?"

"Traci, don't be dramatic. Houston isn't the middle of nowhere. It's a vibrant city, and is where I lived when I was your age. Besides, Richard isn't just some guy. He's the most incredible man I've ever met. He's literally a hero, and we're lucky to have him in our lives. You're going to be fine."

"I'm not going to be fine, because I'm not going." I was unsuccessfully trying to hold back tears. What about David? What about my friends?

"Honey, listen. I know you're upset. But you are going with us, and the sooner you accept that, the sooner you can get excited about the move."

"I am not going, and I am not ever going to be excited to move to Texas! Can't I just move back to Arizona?"

"Traci, your father is busy with his new wife and kids. You don't really have a choice about this. I'm sorry you're upset, but you'll get over it. You can make new friends in Texas." With that, she got up and left the room.

"And this is your room for now." My mom stood in the hallway of a dark, furnished apartment, pointing at a room next to the bathroom. "Remember, we are only staying here for two weeks until the new house is ready. But we'll get you registered in school and everything on time."

I leaned down to scratch my legs, as the carpet was flea infested.

"Yeah, the exterminators are coming tomorrow. We're having the furniture delivered straight to the new place so that we don't get fleas there." Our new dog Baron was chewing and scratching already.

I didn't even care about the fleas. I didn't care about anything. It had been a long, hot summer in Arizona with my father, and I'd rebelled so hard against any kind of rules that we'd spent the summer fighting and him threatening to send me home.

"I don't have a home!" I shouted to him. I'd gone from being a sweet kid who dreamed of becoming the next Marie Osmond to being an angry teenager who was sneaking alcohol and experimenting with boys. I figured that my parents could force me to move to Texas, but they couldn't control what I did when I wasn't with them.

The plan had been for Chris and me to spend the summer with our father and then come home to the new house all set up. But apparently there was some kind of delay because we ended up in the flea-infested apartment instead. I was miserable. Chris was scared. And our mom was acting like this was some grand adventure. I didn't even like this astronaut guy, but we had changed our whole lives because Mom had fallen in love again.

"We'll see how long this one lasts," I said to my friends before I left Miami.

"Racy. Come here. I want to show you something." Richard was standing in the kitchen holding a plate that I'd just washed.

"What?" I really didn't want to stop watching my show.

"Come here and I'll show you."

"Fine." I shuffled into the kitchen. "What is it?"

"Do you see these dishes?" He was pointing to a stack of plates and bowls and other items that he'd taken out of the dishwasher and placed on the counter.

"Yeah? I just washed them. Why did you take them back out?"

"Because, Traci, if you run the dishwasher with food stuck on like this, it will get dried on."

"Then why do we even have a dishwasher?" I stood there, arms crossed, glaring at him.

He chuckled. "When I was a kid, we didn't. Plus, look at the grease on this pan. That's not going to evaporate."

"Fine. I'll redo them."

"I'll show you how."

The last thing in the world I wanted was for him to teach me anything, but I didn't really have a choice. He rolled up his sleeves, got out another sponge, and started to show me how to wash dishes.

"You see, Racy, the way you do one thing is the way you do everything. It may not seem like a big deal if there's a little grease on the pan or a spot on the glass. But, over time, those small things start to add up, and little messes can become big ones. When Pete and Al were coming back into the ship after having been on the lunar surface, they were absolutely covered in moon dust. I literally told them, 'Holy smokes. You're not getting in here and dirtying up my nice clean command module.' I made them strip down to their birthday suits and hand me the moon rocks, their suits, and everything before I unlocked the seal and let them back in."

"Why? It was just dirt."

"Because we were in an enclosed space with no gravity. That dust was going to get over everything including the instrument panels. You can't exactly use a feather duster up there."

"Yeah, I guess that makes sense." This isn't space, though. It's Texas, I thought, begrudgingly, as I dried the pan with a dish towel.

When he saw my eyes wandering back to the living room and my television show, he added, "Besides, you save a lot of time and hassle if you just do something right the first time."

I didn't agree with him at all. In my thirteen-year-old mind, doing something "good enough" was good enough. But I didn't want to get in trouble or have him keep trying to teach me, so we just wordlessly stood side by side and finished rewashing the dishes.

I'm not going to say that this experience led me to become an amazing dishwasher. In fact, my teenage kids teased me about my terrible dishwashing skills and would often rewash the dishes themselves. But I definitely learned that the way we do one thing is the way we do everything, and that sometimes "good enough" isn't.

3.

Don't Half-Ass It

Give It Your All

"Aren't you supposed to be practicing piano?" My brother Chris didn't even look away from the television as he said this to me. It was a Saturday morning and Chris was hogging the television watching cartoons. Our mom was at her French cooking class, and I was trying to get him to let me watch a show. "I'm gonna tell Mom that you didn't practice."

My parents had gotten me a piano after I'd begged, pleaded, and promised to practice for thirty minutes a day three times a week. Wisely, they'd rented it and told me I had to commit to six months of lessons before they would buy one for me. It turned out, I liked listening to the piano far more than I liked playing it.

Reluctantly, I sat at the piano and half-heartedly messed around. Bear walked behind me with a beverage and a snack to go watch sports on the other television. "Sounding good, Racy. Keep it up!"

Hoping that no one would notice or care that I didn't practice for the full thirty minutes, I slipped off the piano bench and headed toward my bedroom. I could hear the blended sounds of sports and cartoons coming from the two televisions.

"Racy, come here."

I inwardly groaned because I figured he knew how long I'd practiced and was going to give me a lecture on following through on commitments. He was big on that.

"How was piano practice?" He was munching on a chip and handed me one.

"Okay, I guess."

"You didn't play for very long." Before I could answer, he yelled at the referee on television. "That was offsides!"

I didn't know what to say, so I didn't say anything.

"Is it that you don't like to play piano, or you don't like to practice?" he asked, never taking his eyes off the game.

"Both, I guess."

"You know, Racy, you don't have to finish everything you start."

I turned to look at him in shock. What? Captain Commitment and Follow-Through was telling me to quit piano? This had to be some kind of trick. "What do you mean?"

"I mean that not everything you try is going to be something you stick with forever." He took a bite of his sandwich and continued. "Look at these guys," he said, gesturing to the TV. "What do they do for a living?"

"They're football players?"

"Yes. They are professional football players. And they spend a lot of hours practicing to be good enough to be pros. But most of the people who want to be a professional athlete don't make it."

"Because they quit?"

"Yes. But sometimes quitting is the right decision. It's okay to decide you don't like something or aren't good at it and decide to stop. Did you know that I was an executive vice president of the New Orleans Saints for a while?"

"You were?"

"Yeah, it was right after I left NASA. I was supposed to be part of Apollo 18, but they canceled the program at 17. There wasn't a reason for me to stay with NASA anymore, so I retired. My friend

John, who owned the Saints, had been trying to get me on board for years, so when I ran into him at a White House thing, he finally convinced me."

My fourteen-year-old brain was spinning. I didn't know which was more shocking, that he'd been part of a professional football team or that he'd been to the White House.

"Wow," was about all I could think to say. "Did you know anything about football? Other than watching it on TV, I mean?"

"Not really. But I didn't know anything about being an astronaut before I did that either. So I figured it would be an adventure."

"Was it?"

"It was."

"Were you any good at it? Is that why you quit?"

Richard laughed and said, "Well. I was good at parts of it. One of the things I learned in NASA was how to solve problems. And how to deal with people. That's something that pretty much any job requires. So I figured I could take those skills and apply them to sports management."

"Did you go to the Super Bowl?" I was trying to imagine him out on the field with Gatorade being dumped on his head or something.

"No, we didn't. We actually lost more games than we won. After a few years, I started to see that it wasn't where I wanted to invest my time. So I stopped." He turned to look at me, directly, and said, "But I gave it my all while I was there, Racy. I didn't half-ass it."

Suddenly, I got it. Either play the piano and give it my all, or don't. It was okay to quit something, but not until after giving it a real effort.

"You promised your mom and me that you'd give piano six months. Even if you decide to quit and that it's not what you want to do, you have to give it your all for the whole six months. Don't half-ass it."

"So, be a whole ass or no ass at all?" I said, with a smile.

"Hahaha! Right." He reached out and messed my hair. "You are really something, Racy."

4.

I'm Just a Human Being

We're Just Humans Floating on a Rock in Space

It was the fall of 1980, and the presidential election was in full swing. The current president, Jimmy Carter (whom I had a small crush on because of his gentle demeanor, blond hair, and big smile) was going against former actor Ronald Reagan. We'd been talking a lot about it in my eighth-grade social studies class, and I was just starting to get interested in the world around me.

My parents were sitting in the living room watching the news when I wandered in, curious. I plopped on the couch and asked my parents, "Are you guys Republicans or Democrats?"

Now, in normal conversation, this isn't a topic one can ask. It's never a good idea to talk about politics, religion, or sex. But, in this case, I was in my formative teen years, and in between arguing about homework and chores, my folks were probably thrilled I'd asked the question.

"We're Republican," my mother answered. "I was a Goldwater girl back in the day."

Richard laughed and looked at her. "You were? Hell, I'd vote for anybody if you were on their campaign."

"Awww. You." They kissed and I was so grossed out I almost left the room. No teenager wants to see PDA between adults, let alone their parents.

"So, President Carter is a Democrat and Ronald Reagan is a Republican, right?"

"Correct," Richard answered. "Those are the two main parties of our electoral system."

"What's the difference between them?"

From the other room, we were interrupted by my brother yelling. "Mom! Get Baron off my bed. He won't leave and he's getting fur all over my Star Wars blanket." She got up to go rescue the dog and the beloved Luke Skywalker comforter.

"Well," Richard began, "Democrats tend to be more interested in social issues and they believe that the government's job is to take care of its people. They're more about equality and fairness. Republicans tend to be more about individual rights and freedoms and believe the government should be less involved in people's lives than the Democrats do."

"How come you're a Republican? Don't you care about taking care of others?"

"Of course I do. But I was a career military officer and, well, we just tend to be more Republican. There are exceptions of course. That's just a generalization."

"I don't know which one I'm going to be. I can see both sides."

"I'll let you in on a little secret, Racy."

I could hear my mom and brother in the other room, and I was eager to hear his secret so I scootched in closer. "Okay?"

"The truth is, it's all made up. When Pete [Conrad] and Al [Bean] were on the lunar surface, I had a lot of time on my hands to think about things. When I piloted the command module to the back side of the moon [Apollo 12], I was completely and utterly alone. When I came around and saw Earth just sitting there—this blue and white ball floating in space—it took my breath away and brought tears to my eyes.

"Everyone I had ever known—had ever met in my whole life—was down there. From the random gas station attendant to my wife and kids. The only exceptions were Pete and Al, and they weren't with me either. It was an almost unexplainable feeling of aloneness."

Richard had tears in his eyes as he told me this. He extended his left arm and held up his thumb. "I held my arm out like this and closed one eye and was able to block out the whole Earth with my thumb. I could make every human on the planet disappear just by blocking them out with my thumb. It was then that I realized that none of it really matters. Political differences and wars, country lines and divisions. They don't matter. We are all just people sitting on a blue and white ball floating in endless nothingness."

He put his arm down and shook his head. "All the stuff you see on TV? The arguing and fussing? It's bullshit. So, really, when you ask, I'm not a Democrat *or* a Republican. I'm just a human being."

5.

Harmless Fun

Not Every Problem Is Serious

"I can't believe you think that what she did was okay!" This was my mother, yelling at Richard. They were in their room, and I could hear them from mine, which was right next door. "What she did was not okay, and I don't appreciate you siding with her."

"What did you do?" Chris asked, as he came into my bedroom through the Jack-and-Jill connected bathroom we shared.

"None of your business," I said, trying to keep him quiet so I could hear what they were saying.

"But Mom grounded you for a whole month!" Chris replied. "She's going to cancel your birthday party."

The conversation dropped to the point where I couldn't make out what they were saying anymore, but it didn't take a detective to figure it out. They were fighting over the fact that I'd snuck out early that morning and my friends and I had "TPed" another girl's house. The girl's parents had apparently seen us and called the parents of the girls who'd done the damage with the toilet paper, and my mom was outraged.

"How dare you sneak out of this house and vandalize property!" she said when she hung up the phone. "Get in your room while I figure out what to do with you."

As my brother noted, she did intend to ground me for a month and said that my fifteenth birthday at the amusement park AstroWorld would be canceled. "You don't deserve it," she said.

When Richard came home that evening and my mom told him what I'd done, it looked to me like he was trying to hold back a grin. "Cookie," he said, using her nickname in an effort to calm her down, "it's just harmless fun." He went into their room to change, and she followed him in and kept yelling at him.

"It's not harmless fun. It's the first step into a life of crime."

I could hear him laughing. "A life of crime? I see where Traci gets her dramatic streak."

Chris and I had never heard them fight before, and he was too young to remember the screamers our mom used to have with our father. But Chris's huge brown eyes looked scared. "Do you think we're going to move again?"

I didn't think so, but given our mom's history, you never knew what could happen. They were planning on being married a few days before my birthday party. Would she cancel that too?

We just stayed in my room talking about stuff until we heard the tones change from angry to calm. Then we heard a knock on my door. It was Richard. "Can I come in?"

The door opened and he said, "Chris, I need to talk to your sister for a few minutes. Can you go in your room, please?"

As Chris walked to his room and shot me a sympathetic look over his shoulder, I'm not gonna lie. I was pretty nervous. Richard had a serious look on his face.

"So, your mom told me what happened," he said, plopping down into my bean bag chair. "How do you even sit in this thing?" he muttered. "Tell me your version."

"So, Autumn and I got mad at this girl for . . . something . . . and so I told Mom that I wanted to help decorate for the pep rally at school this morning and wanted to get there early. She said no, so I climbed out my window and went anyway. But instead of going to the school, we went to her house and threw rolls of toilet paper up into the trees in front. We wanted to do it in the morning so that the sprinklers would soak it all in."

"I see. What did the girl do that was so bad?" he asked, clearly holding back a grin.

I sat there for a minute because I didn't want to tell him. "She was talking to a guy at lunch."

"And I'm guessing this is a boy you like?"

I nodded.

He took a deep breath and brushed a stray hair off his brow as he tried to readjust himself in the bean bag.

"Okay, Racy, I'm going to tell you a story that I think you're old enough to hear now. I just told your mom the same thing in the hopes that she'd lighten up on you. Because, even though you lied to your mom and snuck out, and TPing someone's house isn't a particularly good choice, it's pretty harmless in the grand scheme of things."

My teenage ears were perked up. A story that I was old enough to know now? What could it be?

"So whenever there are astronauts that are trained to go on a mission, they always train backup astronauts who can step in if something happens, and someone gets sick or can't participate in the mission for some reason. On Apollo 12, that person was Dave Scott.

"Well, Dave is a serious prankster, and he pulled off what is likely to be the best one in the history of the space program."

"Really? What did he do?"

"When we were up there, we had a lot of tasks to complete. Experiments and scientific samples—just a lot of stuff. When Pete and Al were on the lunar surface, there were checklists attached to their wrists. They were also wearing microphones, and everyone at Mission Control could hear what they were saying.

"So, at one point, Pete and Al just burst out laughing. I couldn't imagine what was so funny, and it actually seemed out of context to the point where I was worried that there was something wrong with them. They seemed to calm down, but never said a word about what was so funny."

"Did you ever find out?"

He laughed, "I sure as hell did. While they were still down on the surface, I opened a locker and what did I see? A photo of a topless Playboy Playmate with a suggestive comment on it. I burst out laughing, too, and figured that Dave had planted it, and pulled off something similar with Pete and Al."

"What did he do to them?"

"He snuck X-rated photos of other Playmates onto the checklists that were on their arms."

"And you never said anything?"

"No! Our conversations were being broadcast live across the world. We didn't think the American people would appreciate naked pictures being stowed aboard a very expensive rocket ship paid for with tax dollars." Richard was chuckling at the memory.

"So what happened to it?"

"I still have it. Maybe someday I'll auction it off or something, but for now it's one of my favorite possessions."

"Can I see it?"

"Hahaha, no you can't. But I told your mom about it just now and explained that what you did isn't exactly the beginning of a life of crime. It really was just a harmless prank."

"What can I do, though? She already grounded me and took away my party."

Richard was struggling to get out of the bean bag chair. "Go talk to her, Racy. Tell her you're sorry for lying and sneaking out and that you didn't mean any harm and that you won't do it again." He looked at me meaningfully. "You won't do it again, right?"

I nodded my head.

"Maybe she'll shorten your sentence and let you have that party."

Years later, in 2011, he did auction that photo off. I was in my late thirties before I ever saw it. (It seems so harmless compared to today's images!) My mom did back down, grounded me for two weeks instead of a month, and gave me back my birthday party. And despite Chris's fears that we would have to move out, Richard and our mom were married on May 17, 1981.

6.

California Here We Come

Happy Wife, Happy Life

For pretty much my entire life, National Lampoon's *Vacation* has been one of my favorite movies. In fact, I love pretty much any road trip movie, largely because of the amount of traveling we did when I was a kid. But even Chevy Chase couldn't have handled our 1,600-mile road trip from Kingwood, Texas, to Palos Verdes, California.

Let me set the scene. A couple of weeks after the wedding, we packed up and moved to California so that Richard could take a new job. I was not unhappy in the least to be leaving Texas, as I was fifteen and just starting my sophomore year in high school.

We had movers for our furniture but decided to make a family road trip over three days to drive from Texas to California. Three long days in a car with a guy who expected military precision from the journey.

But he was in *our* family now.

The car was a black 1976 Chevy Monte Carlo (which later became my first car). A classic "pimp mobile" with a peeling vinyl top and small side windows that didn't open. It was a two-door, which meant that in order to enter and exit the vehicle, everyone in front had to get out and pull the seat up so that the occupants in back could get out. Those of us in the back were basically trapped and cramped. Now, I'm five feet tall, and if I was cramped, you know it was crowded back there.

It was June 1981, and this new family of five (including Baron, our Doberman) and our belongings were crammed into the car. The black car with the vinyl top absorbed the stifling Texas heat. That car was so hot that it was like traveling inside a barbecue.

"I'm cold," I said, freezing in the back. Richard had the air conditioner set so low that it was more like being inside a refrigerator inside a moving barbecue. Even the dog was shivering.

"Dick, can't you turn up the temperature a bit?" My mother looked at Richard with a glare. "It really is cold in here."

He just drove on, gripping the wheels with his white knuckles, poised at ten and two, with his lips pressed together so tightly that they practically disappeared.

"Can't we listen to something other than talk radio?" I asked. The batteries on my Walkman died miles ago and we were all forced to listen to the radio.

Silently, he banged a button on the car radio, and a ballgame came on. It wasn't exactly what I wanted to hear, but we all knew better than to ask him to change it again.

"Traci! Put Baron on your side of the car. His fur is itching me!" Chris tried to shove the dog over to me.

"No, he's been leaning on me all day. It's your turn." I shoved him back over to Chris's side. The dog was taller than both of us, and we spent the next ten minutes shoving him back and forth.

"Ew, what's that smell?" my mom asked. "It has to be coming from the inside of the car because the windows are hermetically sealed." She glared at her new husband and then turned around to look at us. "Chris, did you take your shoes off?"

"I think it's the dog. He farted," Chris said, holding his nose.

"Gross! Mom! We need to pull over. I think he needs to poop."

"Dick. Can't we just stop for a break?"

"Linda, listen. We have a very tight travel schedule, and if we don't keep up the pace, we'll get off-track. We've already had our morning and afternoon breaks. We'll stop in—" he peered at the odometer, "—157.3 miles."

"Dick, that's two and a half hours from now. I don't think the kids or the dog can wait that long."

"Fine." He gripped the steering wheel even tighter, and I started to notice the cars and landscape whizzing by in a blur. Instead of stopping, he was speeding up!

"Richard! What are you doing? Slow down! You're going to get us killed." My mom was gripping the seatbelt.

Through gritted teeth he said, "I am not going to get us killed. I happened to have won the Bendix Trophy and broke the transcontinental speed record."

"That was in an airplane! SLOW DOWN."

"Fine." He slowed down to a regular speed but turned the air conditioning up again and put talk radio back on, so loudly that none of us could hear him muttering under his breath.

Little did I know that this road trip would become the basis of some of my fondest memories with Bear.

"Remember that road trip?" I'd say.

"I sure the hell do. Let's just say that it was easier being stuck in the Gemini 11 capsule for three days with Pete, out in space, than it was traveling with your mom, you kids, and a dog with IBS across the country. Never again!"

7.

The Mystery of the Blue Dots

Keep Secrets

The night we arrived in California, it was under the cover of darkness. I'm not sure if this had been planned or if we had gotten off of Captain Gordon's elaborately planned schedule. We spent our first night in a hotel in Palm Springs, which is about two hours outside of Los Angeles.

It had been a long trip, and we were all pretty sick of each other, so as soon as we got to the hotel, we all bolted in different directions. Chris and I were sharing one room, and our parents had another, adjoining room.

"Can we order room service?" Chris asked.

Bear sighed because he was as committed to sticking to a budget as he was to sticking to a schedule. He was about to say no when Mom whispered something in his ear. He grinned and said, "Sure. Why not? But order off the kids menu."

They headed to their room and Chris and I headed next door. After we ordered, I left Chris to wait for the food, and I went down to the pool for a much-needed break.

I was sitting on a deck chair looking up at the stars, listening to my Walkman when I sensed someone next to me.

"Hey, Racy."

"Hey, Bear."

"It's been a pretty long trip, hasn't it?"

"Yeah. I'm kind of nervous though. What if the people in California don't like me?"

"Hahaha, how could they not like you?" I noticed he had his shoes off and thought, not for the first time, that his feet were so white that they looked like they'd never seen the sun. They were literally shaped like shoes.

"You just say that because you're my dad."

"Well. Honestly, honey, being liked is overrated. What matters is that you do a good job, try your best, and if that's not good enough, well, they aren't worthy of you."

I don't know if it was the unfamiliar environment or the fact that he was officially my stepfather now, but I finally got the courage to ask him some of the questions I'd always wondered. I leaned back in my chair, hands behind my head, and we both looked at the full moon in the desert sky.

"Can I ask you some stuff?"

His eyebrows raised. "What kind of stuff? Boy stuff?"

God no! "No! Space stuff."

"Hahaha, oh sure. Shoot."

I started with the one that I'd been wondering about the most. "What are the blue dots on the sides of your ears?" He had blue dots, like a freckle, but also like an old tattoo, on the side of both ears, where the cartilage is.

He laughed and said, "I could tell you, but then I'd have to kill you. It's classified. Ask me something else."

"Okay, did you really drink Tang in space?"

"Yes, but that was an advertising deal. I liked it though."

"What was your favorite astronaut food?"

"Ice cream. Just like on Earth."

"Was the food good?"

"Not particularly. But it's better than the MREs that deployed troops get, so we didn't complain."

"How did you go to the bathroom in space?"

"Well, nowadays it's a lot easier. But in the early Apollo days, we basically strapped a collection bag to our asses. And everything was measured. Everything. NASA didn't really know the impact of a gravity-free environment and so they used us as guinea pigs for future astronauts. The kinds of tests they did on us were unreal.

"They took the best of the best, Navy test pilots, and then put us through every imaginable test. They spun us, poked us, trekked us out in the desert. We were sent to jungle survival school, and we learned how to walk on the bottom of a pool. It was crazy, but no one knew what we would find out there."

"Were you scared?"

"Hell yes I was scared. But that didn't matter. I had a job to do, and I focused on doing it. I didn't have time to waste being scared."

I was just about to ask another question when I heard my mom approach. "There you guys are! Chris said you left before your dinner arrived. It's there now."

That was my cue to leave. She had some wine and a couple of towels. This was their honeymoon after all, so I went back to our room and had dinner and watched *Charlie's Angels* with Chris. We left Palm Springs early the next morning to begin our new adventure as a family in California. But, suddenly, I wasn't as afraid to start over in a new school.

Side note: I never learned what those blue dots were. I assume that NASA implanted a recording device into his ears so they could track what he was hearing. But that is literally just a guess on my part. It might have been something as different as a tattoo he got on vacation somewhere. I'll never know. He took that classified information to his grave.

8.

The Monte Carlo Has Landed

A Good Friend Lasts a Lifetime

"Can we go home now?" I was standing on the cliffs of Palos Verdes, looking at the Pacific Ocean for the first time. It was a beautiful sight, indeed. But, much like Clark Griswold and his family standing in front of the Grand Canyon, my appreciation of the natural California coastline was short-lived. We had just driven from Palm Springs, stopping only to get the car washed, and hadn't even been to the new house yet.

"Look! Kids! Those are dolphins!" My mother had her hand at her brow and was peering into the distance.

"How cool!" Chris exclaimed.

"I think that's a good sign, Cookie. This is going to be a good place for us." Richard put his arm around my mom and the three of them stood looking at the horizon.

I was standing by the car, ready to go see my new room. I didn't care about dolphins and signs. I just wanted to get away from the family and go check out our new pool.

I didn't realize until many years later that the reason he was so taken by the beauty of the sea was because he'd seen it from space. I read a quote in the *Washington Post* [Nov. 8, 2017] once, where he said, "The Earth is the only thing out there that looks like that's the place you ought to be because it exhibits a tremendous amount of fragility. The sheer beauty of this planet is awesome. The blues of the oceans, the whites of the clouds and the khaki color, the appearance of the continent. It's awesome. It really is."

"Who is your best friend?" I asked Richard.

We'd been living in the Palos Verdes house for a few months, and I'd made some new friends, but not anyone I'd consider a best friend. I had Kurt, in Lake Havasu, whom I hung out with when I'd go see my father, but he was more like a brother than anything.

"Well, I have a lot of folks I'd consider friends, but I'd have to say Pete is my best friend. We were roommates on the USS *Ranger* and also flew together in Gemini 11 and Apollo 12. But mostly, it's because he's crazy. I've never met anyone more funny or irreverent." He then looked at me and said, "Except maybe your mom."

I didn't know Pete all that well. I just knew him as "Uncle Pete" and the guy that we went to shuttle landings with and who sat at our table during astronaut events. His gap-toothed smile, insanely long eyebrows, and ability to make Richard laugh were his most notable traits to me. Whenever they got together, Pete and Bear and the gang, it was a lot of laughter and fun.

As serious and momentous as the Apollo 11 venture was, Apollo 12 was rowdy and fun. The crew knew that they were a sequel, so to speak, and that they weren't destined to become household names. That afforded them a certain freedom that the first astronaut group didn't have. And that sense of "whoopie" (Pete's words as he became the third man to walk on the moon) lasted well beyond the team's time in the space program.

"So you guys are friends because you share the same sense of humor?" I asked.

"Pete and I share a helluva lot of stuff—including a pretty amazing past. But, no. Pete's my best friend because we respect each other. He's one of the smartest men I've ever known—and that's saying a lot. He's brave, and despite his outgoing personality—some people called us the cockiest men in the space program—he really is humble on the inside. He's a little bit of a rebel, but he was also a good officer. I dunno, Racy. He's just an amazing guy."

He got up and went to the fridge for a beer. Cracking it open, he turned to me and said, "That's what you want to hold out for in a friend. Someone who you respect and who brings out the best in you. Someone you can have fun with, but someone who literally has your back when you need it."

I took those words to heart, and later that year when I met Pam, the woman who would be my best friend until we were almost fifty years old, I was able to recognize a good friendship when I saw one.

9.

“The Scariest Thing I Ever Did”

Everyone Fails

“I am not getting back into a car with her, Dick.” My mother stood at the curb with her hands on her hips. “I value my life too much to risk it trying to teach a crazy person to drive when she won’t listen to me.”

I was at the wheel of the Monte Carlo and there was a fresh dent on the rear panel from when I’d clipped a corner too tightly. In my defense, I’d only had my driver’s permit one week and really didn’t have a lot of experience. Plus, I was five feet tall and could barely see over the steering wheel. And I might have not been all that accepting of my mother’s feedback while in the vehicle.

"You teach her. I'm not going to do it." My mom went back into the house, leaving me in the car and Richard standing in our driveway.

"Well, Racy. I guess it's me or nothing." He opened the passenger door and got in.

I hadn't wanted him to teach me. I didn't want anyone to teach me, honestly. I was rebellious and defensive and took even the slightest suggestion as a personal criticism. But, back in the day, you needed a parent to teach you how to drive. So Bear was it.

He saw the look on my face and said, "It's not gonna be so bad. Really. I taught guys how to fly planes. And I taught my other kids to drive. As they say in Texas, this ain't my first rodeo."

The problem was, it was *my* first rodeo.

"Okay, so you turn the car back on. Yeah, like that. Then signal. No, to the left." He leaned over and looked. "No, your *other* left."

I glared at him.

"Okay now pull out into the street. Slowly. SLOWLY. Traci. Slow down!"

I slammed on the brakes.

"Not like that, Traci. Gently."

I was on the verge of tears and he could see it.

"It's okay, Racy. You're fine. Just take a deep breath and accelerate. Slowly."

I did as he said, and we approached a busy intersection, and I looked at him in a panic. "Now what?"

"Okay, now we are going to stop at this stop sign and make a right turn when it is safe to do so. Signal first."

I pulled up to the intersection of Hawthorne Boulevard and our little street. I looked to the left and there was no one coming, so I pulled out into the intersection to make a left turn. Straight into westbound traffic.

"You're supposed to be turning RIGHT! OH MY GOD, TRACI!!!" I swear I heard him screaming.

Several cars slammed on their brakes, screeching and honking. "What are you doing?" they yelled. "Get off the road!"

"Just pull over into this parking lot, Traci." His voice sounded a little shaky. "I'll take it from here."

We got out of the car and changed places. I was barely holding on from panic, embarrassment, and frustration.

Richard took a deep breath and looked at me, shaking his head. "Traci. I have had my ass strapped to a rocket ship that they then SET ON FIRE. I was shot into SPACE, struck by lightning TWICE. And I can honestly say, teaching you to drive is hands down the scariest thing I have ever done in my life. Let's find you a driving school that has a lot of insurance."

A few days later, we were on our way to Home Depot for something, and Richard said, "I noticed that when your mom and I were teaching you to drive, it was hard for you when you did the wrong thing."

I started to feel embarrassed and ashamed again, but just said, "Well, who isn't upset when they mess up?"

He laughed and said, "True. True. But, Racy, learning to drive is a lot like training to become an astronaut. Except there's a huge difference. There are a lot of other drivers out there and people who know how to do it well. When we were training for Gemini and Apollo, no one really knew how to do it and we made a lot of mistakes. Sometimes the mistakes were preventable, but sometimes they weren't. When we were doing EVAs—extra-vehicular activities—we didn't have a good system of feedback so that folks like me could be aware of the problems of the guys that came before me. I didn't even find out about a lot of it until much later when there were books written about it."

"So you made mistakes in space?"

"There were some problems, yes. And, I want to tell you, Racy, it was very frustrating to deal with. I was wearing this pressurized suit and had to put this visor on the helmet. But we hadn't practiced it in a real zero gravity environment, of course. So, it didn't go well. Then, when the hatch popped open, I just started floating off because we hadn't learned to put hand or foot rails on the ship. I had to use my legs to basically hold on while I was doing the EVA. I began to get really fatigued and I was sweating and my heart rate was rising."

"What happened?"

"We ended the EVA. Pete later said that it was the scariest experience he ever had, watching me out there."

"Because of your friendship?"

"Yeah. Imagine if your best friend were in trouble and you couldn't go help her. We were trained to 'cut loose' one of us if something had gone wrong. But I knew I could never leave Pete or Al on the moon, and they knew they wouldn't just leave me to float off into oblivion. Luckily, it didn't happen, and we never had to make that choice."

I nodded as we pulled into the Home Depot parking lot.

"Anyway, the whole world watched me fail at the EVA. It was frustrating and not a little embarrassing. But the thing is, Racy, you can't get an ego about it. Everyone fails. Everyone messes up. And it's hard to learn and try new things. It's not personal, though. You just learn from it, and move on."

I'd love to say that this pearl of wisdom helped me learn to drive more peacefully and allowed me to receive feedback in an open-hearted manner. But I was fifteen and didn't really learn that lesson for another fifteen years. I did become a pretty good driver in the end, though.

10.

Challenging Authority

Don't Go Along with Things That You Know Are Wrong

"Traci, guess what?" My mom sat down next to me on the couch, holding a piece of paper in her hand. "I just entered this!"

She handed me the flier. "You entered a bikini contest?"

"Yes! Can you believe it? I'm thirty-seven years old and I'm going to be competing against a bunch of twenty-somethings!" She flexed her bicep. "Feel how strong I am."

We had been working out together at the Nautilus gym for a few months. She, admittedly, had a head start, as she never really had a weight problem. I, on the other hand, was quite a bit more "curvy."

"Why?" I asked, as I felt her strong bicep. "And why do it at a bar?" The contest was at a local establishment, Pancho and Wong's. We would often go there for their Mexican-Asian fusion food, and they also had a lively bar scene. I had just turned sixteen, so I wasn't allowed into the bar part of the restaurant.

"Because, Traci, that's where it's being held! It's this Saturday. Come with me!" Her big blue eyes were filled with excitement.

"I can't. I have to work." I'd taken a job at a clothing store in Torrance.

"Call off. It will be fun!"

Granted, the idea of spending the day at Pancho and Wong's was far more appealing than spending the day rehanging clothes that people left all over the floors of the dressing rooms. So, I said, "I'll ask for the day off."

Apparently I was such a valued member of the team that my boss couldn't live without me, and she declined my request to take Saturday off.

Saturday arrived and I was in the kitchen eating breakfast before my mom took me to work (I still hadn't gotten my driver's license yet).

"Traci. Seriously. Come with me today. Just don't go to work." My mom had a mischievous glint to her eyes. "When in your life are you going to see your mother compete in a bikini contest? Versus a minimum wage job you probably won't even remember having."

"Mom, I'll get fired."

"No you won't. We'll handle it."

"I'm sixteen. I can't get into the bar."

"You'll be with your parent. I'll show you how. It's not like you're going to be drinking or anything. You just want to come and support your mom."

The one thing about Linda was that she was very persuasive when she wanted something. Reluctantly, I said, "Okay."

She leaned in conspiratorially and said, "Let's not mention this to Bear. He's off playing golf all day and is, as he would put it, not on a need-to-know basis."

Okay, so we were going to have me blow off work, sneak me into a bar, keep it from Bear, all so she could compete in a bikini contest?

This sounded like heaven to a rebellious sixteen-year-old.

A couple of hours later, we pulled into the parking lot of Pancho and Wong's. "Okay, Traci. Now, when you lie, your face gives it away. I can always tell, because your eyebrows go up, like this." She demonstrated. "So let's get some makeup on you, you wear this hat, keep your eyebrows low, and

I'll distract the bouncer and you just walk in when he's not looking."

"What if it doesn't work?" I asked.

"It will."

What Linda wanted, Linda got, and sure enough, I breezed right in as she was asking the bouncer where the bikini contest entrants were supposed to go.

It was a long, fun day, and my mom came in second place. She was so proud of that, and told the story for the rest of her life how she came in second in a bikini contest when she was almost forty.

"Linda." A patron of the bar went up to my mom. "Let me buy you dinner to say congrats."

"Oh, I can't. I have my daughter here."

"*That's* your daughter? Well, that's fine because I'm with a group of friends. We're over here."

She looked at me. I really didn't want to go because it was nighttime now and I just wanted to call Pam and tell her about my day.

"Sure. But just something quick," she said, as she made her way over to their table.

I guessed I was following, and went along.

It was close to 10:00 p.m. when we finally got home. To say Richard was angry was an understatement. He was fuming.

"Where the hell have you been?" he said, as we pulled into the driveway. "I was worried sick about you." (This was before we all had cell phones.)

My mom turned to me and said, "Traci, go to your room. I'll handle this."

I was not about to stick around for this, so I did as she said. I could hear them arguing loudly and finally there was silence. I fell asleep, wondering what the fallout would be.

The next day, I got a call from my boss. As I predicted, I was being fired for not showing up to work.

"Tell them you got into a car accident," my mom whispered.

I did, and my boss relented. I was to come in that afternoon.

"Here's what we'll do. Let's use makeup to give you a black eye and you tell them that we had a car accident on the way to work and you ended up at Torrance Memorial. You're fine, but you forgot to call. Got it?"

I nodded, uncomfortable with the whole thing. But, she was my mom, so it had to be okay, right?

"Oh, and keep your eyebrows down when you say it."

In the end, her makeup job was convincing, and I got away with the lie and kept my job. But it really didn't feel right.

I hadn't had a conversation or even really seen much of Richard for the next few days. My guess was that this was a pretty big fight between them.

Finally, one afternoon as I was sitting on the couch doing homework, he came in and sat down next to me.

"Hey, Racy."

"Hey, Bear." Was he mad at me? Was I in trouble?

"So I've had some time to calm down after you and your mother's shenanigans this weekend."

I didn't know what to say, so I just waited for him to continue.

He cleared his throat. "The thing is, it can be a hard thing to know when to go against authority and when to comply. This is why we train our military for so long. When you're in an emergency situation, there isn't time to have a conversation about which action to take. The commanding officer makes that call. There were a lot of times in NASA where I didn't agree with the decision made on the ground. But it wasn't my call to make."

"Okay?" I still didn't see where he was going with this.

"But, Racy, it's also important to not go along with things that you know are wrong. Even when they come as an order—or a request—from some-one in authority."

Oh, I get it now.

"I wasn't even mad at your mom about the bikini contest. She's a beautiful woman and I'm proud of her for that. I get why she entered, although I do wish she'd told me about it. The thing I was mad about was her involving you. You are a minor child and that was not an environment you should have been in. She never should have brought you there."

"But it was fun. And nothing bad happened."

"I'm sure it was fun. But something bad did happen. You got away with lying. Trust me, Traci. A person can only get away with that stuff for so long before you get caught. But even more important than that is that you know that it was wrong. You do. And being able to stand up to authority—even your mom—when you're being asked to do some-thing wrong, well, let's just say I hope you make a better choice next time. You're my baby girl and I hate to think of what could have happened to you."

"So, I'm not in trouble?"

"No. I just want you to think about what we talked about today. Remember to live your life according to your values, even if it makes you unpopular."

"I will, Bear." We hugged, and he went to watch golf on TV.

11.

No Dog Left Behind

Never Leave Someone in Peril

"Can you take the dog for a walk before you go to Pam's?" My mom was in the kitchen making lunch for Bear and Chris.

I'd finally gotten my driver's license, and my parents had given me the Monte Carlo to have as my first car. While I was grateful to have a car at all, we were living in a wealthy community and the other kids at school were driving new BMWs and Porsches. Nothing says, "I don't belong here" more than driving up to school in your 1976 pimp mobile with the peeling vinyl top and a dent in the back and parking it next to the Mean Girls and their cars.

Fortunately, I'd befriended Pam, whose parents had given her a monstrous old Cadillac as her first car. We may have been living in multimillion-dollar homes with 180-degree views of the Pacific Ocean, but our parents made sure we knew that it was due to their success and not ours. We'd have to earn our own nice things.

I put Baron's leash on him and headed down the street to a park. There were several different routes to get there, and on this morning, Baron told me he wanted to go a way we'd never gone before. At the corner was a house, set very far back on the lot with an overgrown front yard.

Baron was a beautiful, sweet, shy, black Doberman Pinscher whom we lovingly called Baron Von Hinterbisen, which they told me meant "Baron the Bottom Biter." I later found out that he was Richard's dog from before we met him. Baron was a lover and not a fighter, and when his ears perked up and the hackles stood up at the back of his neck, I was alerted.

"Woof!" he said, staring into the overgrown yard.

A dog yelped at us from behind the fence. It didn't sound normal to me, so we went over to investigate.

"Woof!"

"Yelp!"

"What is it, Baron? What do you see?" Baron was digging, trying to get in the gate.

We walked a little farther and saw the dog. He was a beautiful red Doberman and he was chained to a shed in the backyard. He didn't appear to have any food or water, and while it wasn't overly hot, it was clear the dog wasn't happy.

"Hello?" I said. "Is anyone home?" I was looking for a door to the gate. I didn't see anyone, and Baron and I found the door to the gate and it was unlatched. I tied Baron up outside the gate and slipped inside to investigate.

"Hey, hey buddy. Are you okay?" The dog looked skinny and scared and had his ears back. "You don't have any water!"

I was looking around for a water dish for him when I heard a voice. "What the hell are you doing?" It was a mean-looking old man.

"Your dog doesn't have any water," I said, heart pounding. Baron heard the commotion and started barking to protect me.

"What the hell difference does it make to you? He's my dog and you're on my property. Get out or I'll call the police."

I have no idea what came over me or who the person is who said the following words, but

I answered, "Go ahead and call them. You're the one who'll get arrested for animal abuse."

I stood there, hands on my hips, channeling Linda Gordon, and glared at him.

"Fine, then. You know what? You think it's so easy to take care of a dog? YOU take him." The man went over, unhooked the dog, and handed me the leash. "Just don't come back." He stomped into his house and slammed the door.

What the hell had just happened? I'm standing in some crazy old man's backyard, holding the leash of some dog who'd just been given to me. What was I going to do with him? What would my parents say?

I took the dog out of the yard, and Baron was looking at me like I was crazy. "I know, buddy," I said.

Now I just have to figure out how to get two Dobermans, who don't know each other, home and explain it to my folks.

We went back a block or so, and I tied the new dog to a fence post, and Baron and I jogged the short distance home. I put him in the garage, jumped in my car, and went back for the second dog.

He was terrified that he'd been abandoned, and when I drove up, I could barely get him in the car.

"Come on, guy. Get in the car. Up here. You can do it." Finally I got him in and drove home.

I drove up to the driveway, and my mom was out front, watering the flowers. I'll never forget the expression on her face when I opened the car door and a different Doberman got out.

"Where's Baron?" she asked.

I explained the story and asked if we could keep the second dog. She told me that we'd have to talk to Bear, but that she was okay with it if he was.

"So he just gave you the dog?" Richard asked, a few minutes later.

"Yes!"

"I'm going to have to go talk to him. Can you show me where he lives?"

We jumped in Bear's car and drove the short few blocks to the house. "It's here."

I stayed in the car and watched as Richard went to the door and rang the bell. It seemed like forever, but finally the old man opened the door. I could see them talking, and the old man went from defensive and angry looking to sad. I saw Richard nod his head, the men shook hands, and he walked back to the car.

"Well, Racy. I guess you have yourself a dog."

I was ecstatic! "Thank you!"

"I guess his wife died not too long ago and the dog was hers. He just couldn't handle things after she died and the dog was a reminder of her."

I was only half listening. I had my own dog!

"Can we name him Shed?"

"Yes. But, he's your responsibility. You'll need to walk him and feed him and get a job to buy his food. And, if he doesn't get along with Baron, we'll need to rehome him. Agreed?"

"I promise."

"Oh, and Racy?"

"Yeah?"

"I'm proud of you. You did the right thing rescuing that dog. In the military, we had a 'no man left behind' policy. Even when I was on Apollo, my greatest fear of being alone in the capsule was not that I'd go floating off into oblivion, but that I wouldn't make it back to get Pete and Al and bring them home to their families. It was my job to get them home safely, and it was one I took very seriously. You showed that today, and I am very proud of my baby girl."

We had Shed for several months. He didn't get along with Baron, and after taking two dogs on two walks every day, spending half my minimum wage paycheck on dog food, and working to get them to get along, we agreed to find Shed a good family where he could be the only dog.

The experience—and Bear's pride in me—led me to be the person who has rescued all of her animals off the literal street, in honor of our "no dog left behind" policy.

12.

Lighten Up, Cap'n Fuzzybuns

There's a Difference Between Irreverence and Disrespect

One of the things that happens when you blend two families is that there is often a culture clash. In our case, Mom marrying a military officer/astronaut meant that we were introduced to a world that we knew nothing about—the military culture.

My father and mother had started a radio station in 1970, and then she had gone on to her own career in broadcasting. We knew nothing at all about the military or the protocols expected of the family members. As such, we were rather irreverent about it all.

"They're all so serious," my mom said one day as we were on a family outing to the local commissary, referring to people in uniform. "Why does it all have to be so serious?"

"Listen up," Richard said. "When we get on base, I want you all to behave." He looked at my mom and said, pointedly, "Especially you, Cookie."

He went on. "I am a retired captain in the Navy and people expect to see a certain decorum from my family. This is our first time in this environment, and I want it to go well. Do we understand?"

My mother had an impish grin. "Yes, sir, Cap'n Fuzzybuns. We understand." I wasn't sure how she came up with that nickname for him, and didn't want to think too hard about it.

We pulled onto base and people were literally saluting him. "Captain Gordon, sir."

Sir? The guy who sits in his boxers, snores like a lawnmower, gags while brushing his teeth, and yells at the TV? They're saluting and calling him sir? I had to laugh. There was no way I was going to call him sir. Ever.

The commissary, for those who don't know, is basically a huge grocery store, like Costco, located on military bases with heavy discounts and no tax for members of the armed forces and their families.

Richard was in his element. Walking tall, nodding and saluting, being acknowledged for his rank. We, on the other hand, followed behind him, giggling at the whole scene.

"Oh, Cap'n Fuzzybuns," my mom yelled loudly. "Make sure you get some bread for your tuna sandwiches." He walked faster, turning to glare at her.

"Oh, Bear," I chimed in. "Bear?" He walked faster, ahead of us. "Can we get some chips?" He pretended not to hear us.

Later, on the way home, he was so mad that the veins were popping out on his forehead. "That's the last time I ever bring you people to the commissary. You embarrassed me."

My mom rubbed his arm and said, sheepishly. "We're sorry. Aren't we, kids?" She turned back and winked at us.

"Yes. We're sorry. SIR." And then we all burst out laughing.

We did go back to the commissary—often. And we behaved. We really did understand the difference between fun irreverence and actual disrespect. He taught us the value of protocol and ceremony, and we taught him that it's okay to lighten up, sometimes.

13.

Falling Asleep in Space

Handle Disappointment Graciously

"Do you think he would mind if I asked him some questions?" My oldest friend Kurt was visiting me from Arizona. He and I had been friends ("brother from another mother/sister from another mister") since 1978, and he'd come out to take me to my junior prom.

"No, he's pretty open about his space experiences. Go for it."

"How did you sleep in space?" Kurt asked Richard one evening during the visit.

"Very well, thank you." He chuckled. "I can sleep anywhere."

"Tell them about your nap in space," my mom said, from the kitchen.

"Haha, okay, Cookie. It was my second EVA and this was far more relaxing than the first. My job was to capture some UV pictures of empty space or black voids. They did research on those photos later. But the images had to be taken at night, and Pete had to maneuver the spacecraft into a specific position for me to get the right angle in darkness.

"So, I'm in the hatch, in the pressurized suit, tightly tethered to the ship. You get this kind of warm, fuzzy feeling and it's so peaceful and serene. Half my body, from the thighs up," he said, slapping his thighs, "were outside the ship. When the night side pass of Earth was up, we just had to wait until the Earth rotated through daylight and back to night again. There wasn't much to do, and I kind of drifted off to sleep.

"The next thing I hear is somebody on the ground talking in my ear and Pete going, 'Hunh?' because he'd fallen asleep too."

"You both fell asleep?" Kurt asked.

"Haha, yes. It was a long trip and there was a lot of work to be done. We were tired."

"Is this when you took that Earth rise photo?" Kurt asked, gesturing to the photo we had on the wall of every house I lived with Bear in.

"Yup. A pretty good shot, if I do say so myself."

"Was it hard not getting back to the moon?"

"It sure was, but it was just one of those things. It wasn't personal. Even when it came to who was gonna be the first group to go to the moon. Deke [Slayton] had a rotation system set up long before Apollo was even a program. You were the prime, backup, prime if you stayed on that crew. And in my case, that's exactly the way it happened. Backup on Gemini 8, prime in 11, backup on Apollo 9, prime on 12. Backup on Apollo 15. I was supposed to be prime on 18, but there wasn't one."

"How come you say it *jiminy* instead of *gemin-eye*."

"I dunno. That's just how we said it at NASA."

"What's the hardest thing, other than not getting to go back to the moon?" Kurt asked, as my mom was setting the dinner table.

"Nothing about it was really hard. I was there to do a job and my focus was on doing the job to the best of my ability. My workplace had a really good view, but it was a working mission."

"Except he's the astronaut no one remembers," my mom added. "No one remembers the guy who didn't get out of the ship on the second mission to the moon. I think that's the worst part."

He chuckled as he got up and made his way over to the table. "Cookie, you know I don't care about that. I never wanted to be famous. Besides, when I go places with you, it's unforgettable." He kissed her cheek.

"Unforgettable, that's what you are," he serenaded her as I went downstairs to get Chris for dinner.

14.

Home Depot Is Closer Than the Moon

Trust Is Everything

"We're moving." My mother announced this at dinner one night.

Of course we are, I thought. It was 1983 and I was in the middle of my senior year in high school. God forbid we should stay in a place more than two years. This was our second home in California already.

"Where to this time?" I asked, with more than a little sarcasm.

"We're buying a house. In Manhattan Beach."

"We're moving to New York?" I asked, as my stomach dropped.

"No, Manhattan Beach is in LA. It's about fifteen miles from here. Near the airport."

"Do I have to change schools?" Chris asked.

"Yes, you do. But, Traci," my mom turned to look at me. "Bear and I talked about it and we know you're in your senior year, so we have decided to allow you to commute."

Earlier that year, I'd traded the Monte Carlo for a sweet, but decrepit 1968 Mustang. My parents were furious with me, as I didn't consult them—I just came home one day in a different car.

"Did you even get it checked out by a mechanic?" they asked.

"Well, duh. I'm in auto mechanics class. I know you're supposed to do that." What I didn't tell them was that I'd skipped class to take the car to the mechanic down the street from school before trading the Monte Carlo for it.

I loved driving the Mustang, so the idea of driving back and forth to Palos Verdes every day was more than fine with me. I'd made the car my own, with an "I ♥ Mick Jagger" bumper sticker and some white fuzzy dice hanging from the rearview mirror. Everyone at school knew me as the crazy chick with all the Diet Dr Pepper cans in the back of her blue Mustang, blasting the Rolling Stones. The side door didn't open all that well, and my passengers had to crawl in and out of the window.

"Sweet!" I said with a big grin.

"Now, Racy, there are gonna be some ground rules. You need to keep your grades up, you need to make sure you get to school on time, and you need to come home straight after school. If you don't, we're going to make you change schools. This is a privilege, not a right. We are trusting you to be responsible."

Yeah, yeah. All I knew was that I wasn't going to have to change schools. I couldn't wait to call Pam and tell her.

"How come she gets to stay in her school but I have to change?" Chris wasn't exactly thrilled, as he was in middle school.

"Because I can't drive you to PV every day and pick you up," Mom said. "And Bear is commuting to Lancaster. That's eighty miles each way."

"This is lame!" Chris got up from the table and stomped off to his room.

"You get back here!" my mom called after him.

"Let him go, Cookie. He needs to blow off some steam." Richard turned back to me. "Now the thing is, we need your help. Your mom and I are scheduled to go to Korea right at the time of the closing. I'm giving a talk, and my son Rick is stationed there. So we're going to be gone for the closing."

"What does that mean? Closing."

"It's when we officially get the house. We need you to get the keys from the Realtor and open up for the movers. You can choose which of the smaller bedrooms you want. Oh, and my son Tom is going to be moving in with us for a while."

I didn't really remember meeting any of Richard's other kids before. They weren't too happy when he married my mom, and so we weren't exactly the Brady Bunch. And when Richard's son Jimmy was killed in a car accident a couple of years before, I never really felt comfortable asking about his other kids. Needless to say I was very surprised that one of them was coming to live with us, let alone one who was in his mid-twenties.

How big is this house? I wondered. They were going to let me choose my room, and there would be room enough for Chris and Tom and my parents' room? Turns out, it was a normal-sized three-bedroom house, and Tom slept on an air mattress on the floor of my brother's bedroom.

"It's over there, Dick. Make a left."

"I think I know where Home Depot is, Linda." Bear was gripping the steering wheel, lips sucked in, and mad.

"Do you, though?" she retorted, glaring at him.

We were on the way to get some packing supplies and, as usual, we were lost. This was before GPS and cell phones. The funny thing was, despite being the navigator on Apollo 12 and making it all the way to the moon, Richard was terrible with directions. We used to tease him that the only reason he made it to the moon was because he could see it.

"Just pull over and get out the *Thomas Guide*. We're lost."

"We are not lost. It's called a detour. That construction back there got us turned around." He was furrowing his brow and looking left and right, and I was beginning to worry that this "detour" was going to spark a fight and I'd be stuck in the backseat listening to it. Their arguments were legendary.

"It's right there!" I exclaimed, pointing to the orange sign just behind some tall buildings. "Right over there." The tension in the car palpably drained.

"See, Cookie. I told you I knew where it was. You just need to learn to trust me."

She glared at him meaningfully and I just stared out the window, eager to get boxes and start packing.

"So you have the keys to an empty house and your parents are in Korea?" My friend Katie looked at me with a mischievous glint in her eye. I didn't have a lot of friends in school, but Katie was on the basketball team, and she had friends.

"Yeah, but they are coming back Sunday."

"That's plenty of time. Let's have a party."

I loved the idea of having a party. What harm could people do? There was no furniture in the house because we hadn't moved in yet. "Yes!"

The new house was in Manhattan Beach (fifteen miles from our high school), and Katie and I could only score one beer each from my parents' fridge or else they'd notice. Unsurprisingly, with no alcohol and the distance from home, no one came to the party. Katie and I sat in the empty living room and drank our one beer and "wrote" our nicknames on the new carpet with our socks. "Boom Boom" and "Moose" had the saddest party ever.

That Sunday, after my parents got home and had gone to check out the new house, they came into my room and my mom said, "I see you had a party while we were gone."

How did she DO that? I wondered. "No, I *tried* to have a party but no one came." I figured honesty was the best policy.

"Really? Then what about the beer cans in the trash? Who's Moose?" She stood there, hands on hips, accusingly.

"Moose is Katie."

"Sure she is, Traci. I don't believe you for one second. You almost got away with it, but you aren't clever enough to lie convincingly."

"I swear! We didn't have a party! It was just us."

"Well, regardless, you proved that we can't trust you. Because of that, you're now getting the smaller room in the house. The one we were going to give to Chris. He's getting the one with the balcony."

"What? That is totally unfair!" I looked at Richard for support. "Bear! Tell her. I shouldn't be punished for *not* having a party!"

He just shook his head and said, "Trust is everything, Racy."

15.

Grow the Hell Up

Sacrifice for a Greater Goal

It was 1984 and Richard was commuting 160 miles a day to and from work. He was launching a startup (although I had no idea at the time what he did for a living, I just knew he was gone all the time). Tom moved in, and he and my mom got into these late-night deep, philosophical conversations. I, too, was commuting to and from school and was gone a lot.

One evening, I heard shouting coming from my parents' room. My room was right next to theirs, and the walls of the new house were pretty thin.

"I'm just saying, Dick, that I didn't get married so that I could spend all of this time alone."

"What am I supposed to do, Linda? This is my company. I can't just quit."

Later, I realized that one of the core differences between Richard's first wife, Barbara, and my mother was that Barbara understood that being married to an astronaut meant that she'd be spending a lot of time alone. And she did.

There are documentaries and books about the astronaut wives and the pressures they faced and the sacrifices they made. Barbara was the one who had to send her husband off to space, with no idea what the impact might be to his health. My stepsiblings were the ones who missed out on their dad being home, who watched the rockets explode and wondered if their dad would be next. But it was Richard's dream and he was committed to it, and his entire family was behind him.

My mom, on the other hand, wasn't exactly the selfless Betty Crocker type, and in the words of a famous song, she "wasn't the kind of girl who liked to be alone."

The strain on their marriage took a toll on the whole family. When he was home, Bear was grumpy and spent a lot of time watching news and sports on TV. When he wasn't home, my mom took out her frustration on me, and we got into huge screaming fights. Chris pretty much stayed in his room or went out with friends. And Tom started dating Cathy, the woman who would later become his wife and one of my closest friends to this day.

That year, the Olympics were in Los Angeles, and the sense of patriotic nationalism was everywhere. As a senior in high school, I was studying both American history and government.

One day, Richard and I were on the couch watching the news and I said to him, "Didn't it bother you that the US spent so much money on the space program when there were so many problems in the country at that time? Everyone called you guys heroes, but the real heroes were folks like Martin Luther King."

The question was straightforward, but my tone was not. He just gave me a sideways glance and said, "It was more complicated than that."

Being seventeen, I couldn't let it go. "Really? It doesn't seem that complicated to me. The whole space program was nothing more than an ego contest between two white men who wanted the bragging rights about who could get to the moon faster. And instead of spending money on poverty and civil rights and correcting what was wrong with America, the government decided to waste their resources on some stupid game of chicken between the US and the Soviets."

He muted the TV and turned to face me. "Is that what they're teaching you in school? That it was an ego contest?"

I panicked a little bit, but stubbornly held firm. "No, that's not what they're teaching. But I can make up my own mind about things. The money should have been spent on solving social problems on this planet, not trying to explore another one."

"First of all, Traci, the moon is not a planet. It's a satellite of this planet." He took a breath in an apparent attempt to calm himself down when talking to a teenager who thought she knew it all.

"Second, you have to realize something. The world you are growing up in is not the world we had back then. The Cold War was raging, and it was dangerous and scary. We had the technology to obliterate the planet and an unstable Soviet leader who might just use it.

"Did you know that Neil [Armstrong, the first person to walk on the moon] went to Russia? Did you know that he left a satchel on the moon with medals commemorating two Russian cosmonauts? The space program was something that brought us together in a time of conflict. Not just one country, but all of them. Eighty percent of the people on the planet watched the Apollo 11 moon landing. Do eighty percent of the people on the planet share a singular experience today?

"If there's one thing I learned out in space it's that we are all on the same planet. NASA was created so that the whole *world* would have a common goal, not just our country. We prided ourselves on transparency. When things went wrong, we learned from it. We talked about it. When the Soviets had problems, they hid it. They lied."

I opened my mouth to speak, but he kept going.

"You have no idea how much teamwork it took to get a man on the moon. Literally hundreds of thousands of people all worked tirelessly to achieve one goal. And every single one of those people, from the guy who made metal bolts to the one who created the communication systems—every single one of them was proud and committed to excellence."

"But—"

"What other social issue can you think of that affects everyone on the planet? I hate to say it, but there will always be problems. There's always going to be war. There will always be poverty. There will always be groups of people who aren't treated fairly. That's just life, Traci.

"The reason we went to the moon wasn't because of ego or nationalism. It was to bring the planet together during a time when social problems were at their worst."

I sat there silently, not sure what to say. But I could see that Richard was angry.

"You have no idea of the sacrifices people made. It took almost half a million people to get us to the moon. Every person sacrificed. I missed so much of my kids' lives. I missed time with my wife. But it wasn't just the astronauts. Everyone did. And, frankly, Traci, I think it's a little entitled of you to sit here in your privilege and think that just because you're learning a little bit about history that you know anything at all about what life was like when you were three years old."

He then grabbed the remote and aimed it at the TV to turn the volume back up.

"I have one piece of advice for you, Racy. Grow the hell up and get some life experience before you start spouting off what you think you know."

16.

Sometimes, You Get What You Need

If You're Going to Lie, Make Sure You Get Away with It

"What do you mean you can't go?" Pam and I were on the phone and I was lying in my bed looking out the window. It was a warm spring day, and the famous Santa Ana winds were blowing hot air.

"My parents are going to be home and they won't let me go."

Pam and I had been invited to a party down the street, and my folks suspected (rightly) that there would be alcohol there. "You're too young for that kind of environment, Traci." This, coming from the woman who took me to a bikini contest at a bar.

"So, sneak out. They'll never know," Pam said.

She had a point. Richard was always tired from the drive and so the folks went to bed early. I knew the code to the alarm and Tom was always out with Cathy. I could easily slip out undetected. "Okay. I'll meet you there at eleven."

Now, Pam still lived in Palos Verdes so she had to drive. But my house was just a block or so away from the party, so I could get there on foot.

"Goodnight!" I said loudly, to my folks, as I closed my bedroom door and waited for 11:00."

"Night Racy!"

I changed into a pair of jeans and my favorite Rolling Stones T-shirt, paused the alarm long enough to slip out a side door, and left my Mustang parked in the driveway. Five minutes later, I was drinking a beer with Pam in the backyard of the neighbors' house.

"Did you have any trouble sneaking out?" she asked.

"No, did you?"

"No, I rolled the car down the street before I started it, so my folks don't suspect a thing."

"Good thing you live on a hill," I laughed.

We stayed at the party for several hours, and then things started winding down. It was close to two in the morning when I said, "Well, I better head back. Drive carefully, Pam." She wasn't much of a drinker and hadn't had more than two beers all night. I could not say the same thing.

I weaved my way down the block, paused the alarm long enough to get in the house, tiptoed up the stairs to my room, and slid into bed still wearing my jeans and T-shirt. The room was spinning and I was looking forward to just going to sleep.

BEEEEP BEEEP BEEEP! The house alarm went off. BEEEEP BEEEP BEEEP!

I heard my parents get up and go turn it off and then come back upstairs. Suddenly, the door to my room flew open.

"So, you're back," my mom said.

Trying to play it off, I yawned and stretched my arms. "What do you mean? I'm sleeping." I rubbed my eyes for effect. "What caused the alarm to go off?"

"Don't give us that bullshit, Traci. You know full well what set the alarm off." My mom was furious.

Richard then looked toward my brother's room and said, "Everything is fine, Chris, go back to bed." Looking back at me, he said, "You woke the whole house up, Traci."

"I have no idea what you're talking about. I have been here the whole time." They can't prove a thing, I thought. I was sticking to my story.

"Really? You sure about that? Then why are you sleeping in full clothes? Why does your room smell like beer? And why did the alarm go off at

10:58 when you left and then again at 2:08 when you got back home?" My mom would have made an excellent cop.

"I don't understand," I said. "How did you know?"

"The wind blew the door open. You didn't close it properly and you set the alarm off when you snuck out," Richard said. He was clearly angry too. "And back in."

"Oh."

"Yeah. Oh. And consider yourself grounded. You'll give your mother the keys to your car and you're taking the bus to school for the next two weeks."

"All the way to PV?"

"Yep. You better get up very early, young lady. It's a long bus ride." Richard turned to me as he headed back to his room and said, "If you're gonna lie, Racy, make sure you get away with it."

They shut my door and I laid back down. My head was still spinning, but this time for a different reason.

"How come he has to take my car?" I whined. I was a week into my bus riding punishment and my mom told me that Richard needed to take my Mustang to work.

"Because the Cadillac is in the shop and your car is just sitting in the driveway."

I was not happy at all, but didn't feel like I could fight it. "Well, can I at least clean it out first?" I wanted to take down the fuzzy dice and get the Diet Dr Pepper cans out of the back.

"Please do," Richard said, from the other room.

I took the bus to and from school, and my car wasn't there when I got home. About an hour later, I heard it pull up and the front door to the house slam.

"Goddammit, Racy. Get down here."

My mom was in the kitchen and when I got there, Richard was red-faced and fuming. "Dick, what happened?"

"What happened? WHAT HAPPENED?" He turned to look at me. "Ask me how my day was."

"Uhhh, how was your day?"

"I get to the parking lot, and the guy at the gate is laughing at me. I park my car in my space. The president of the company's space. People are laughing. I'm wondering what the hell is so funny. I walk down to the office, and my secretary is smiling. 'Morning, Mick.' I ignore it and go into my office. All goddamn day everyone is calling me

Mick. Finally, I go out to get some lunch and I figure it out. Do you know why they were calling me Mick?"

My mom starts to snicker.

"No?"

"Because the car I was driving has a damn I heart Mick Jagger bumper sticker on it. It was humiliating!"

A grin spreads across my face and I sneak a look at my mom, who can barely hold her laughter.

"Well, you know what they say, Dick. You can't always get what you want—"

"—but if you try sometimes, you might just find, you get what you need," I added, laughing.

"You are both crazy, you know that?" he muttered as he stomped up the stairs. "Linda, I'm taking your car tomorrow."

17.

The Family Astronaut

You Can't Rebel Against Authority When You Make the Choice

It's funny how one's parents influence our deepest values, and we aren't even aware of it until much later. Although this book is about my relationship with my astronaut dad, my other dad, Lee Shoblom, was very much a part of my life.

Most men would be intimidated if their ex-wife married an astronaut. They might get a little insecure that an international hero was raising their children. Not Lee Shoblom. My father embraced Richard with open arms and an open home. Maybe it was because he was a broadcasting pioneer and celebrity in his own right. His career brought him to radio and television, introduced him to entertainment stars like Elvis and Tom Jones, coordinating events like MTV's Spring Break, and being inducted into the Broadcasting Hall of Fame. He was personal friends with Senator John McCain and was the person who hired Regis Philbin for his first job.

Or maybe because he was "Daddy Lee" to two little boys, whose own father, "Daddy Greg," was a huge part of their lives. Whatever the reason, Lee Shoblom was secure enough in his role as my father to never, not once, disparage Richard.

I remember numerous family holidays and events, Christmases and birthdays and graduations, where my father introduced Richard as "the family astronaut." I have photos of each dad in the others' house—Richard with my paternal grandmother Doris in Lake Havasu, Lee in the kitchen of our Manhattan Beach house.

"Captain Radio" and Captain Gordon were friends who shared a special bond. Each man knew that he had a special role to play in my life, and that one did not take away from the other.

That attitude about co-parenting influenced how I co-parented with my ex-husbands. It was the norm to invite my exes to birthday parties and holiday celebrations. "I wish I got along with my ex," my friends would say. But it all seemed so normal to me. That was the way I'd been raised.

Shortly before I graduated from high school, my mom had gone away for the weekend on a trip. I don't recall where she went, but I do recall that Bear was home watching us while she was gone.

I was eighteen and had a head full of the independence that I believed came with being a legal adult. Bear and I had done our fair share of arguing and fussing over the years, but one event changed the nature of our relationship permanently. It was, quite ironically, a rock and roll concert.

"Bear," I said, as he sat on the couch. "Pam invited me to a KISS concert at the Forum tonight. Can I go?"

"Did you ask your mom before she left?" he asked, never taking his eyes off the TV.

"No, it's a last-minute kind of thing. And I can't get hold of her." This was before we all had cell phones. "So I'm asking you. Can I go?"

He muted the TV and looked at me. "Honey, look. You and I both know that your mom wouldn't want you going to a concert. It's a school night and I don't think you should go."

"So, you're telling me no?" I felt anger and frustration rising in my belly.

"No, I'm not telling you that. You are an adult and part of being an adult is learning to make your own choices. But you know your mom would say no. I don't want to have to deal with her when she gets back and you probably don't either. So I am asking you as a personal favor to please not go. But it's your call." He turned back to the TV and raised the volume.

I stood there completely shocked. I could go if I wanted to. The choice was mine. I'd never been given that kind of freedom before.

I went upstairs to think about it. If I were going to go, I'd need to call Pam soon. Should I go? I really wanted to see KISS in concert, and it would be way better than sitting at home pretending to do homework.

He was right about one thing, though. My mom would flip her lid if I went. I'd get grounded for sure, but I usually considered being grounded as the price to pay for whatever it was that I wanted to do.

But this was different. You can't rebel against authority if you're given the freedom to make the choice.

It was a tough call. Things were already bad with my mom and Richard, and perpetually bad between her and me. He had never asked me for a personal favor before. Did I want to be responsible for what was sure to be a huge fight between them?

The phone rang. "I got it!" I yelled downstairs. "Hey Pam. Yeah, I can't go. No, Bear didn't say no, but my mom would lose her shit and I don't want to get him in trouble. I'll see you tomorrow at school."

I changed into pajamas and went downstairs to make a snack.

"That what you're wearing to the concert, Racy?" he said, with a twinkle in his eye.

"Naw. I'm not going."

He nodded his head and simply said, "Good call."

Later on, I realized the amount of grace it took for Richard to balance out the family dynamics. He never once tried to take the place of my father; he tried to smooth things out with my temperamental mother and never overstepped the line that she was my parent and he was her husband. When I complimented him on this, he just laughed and said, "It took a whole village to raise you, Racy. I was just part of the team."

Most importantly, that night was the day when we formed an alliance that would last the rest of his life.

18.

Launched into Orbit

Know When It's Time to Go

"You get your ass home right now." My mother was furious with me, as usual.

It was August of 1984. I'd graduated from high school and was working two jobs at different veterinary hospitals. Things had gone from bad to worse with my mom, and I was spending more nights away from home than I was spending at home.

The first time I didn't come home, my mom said, "If you're going to be gone all night, just let us know so we don't worry. Just call, is all we ask."

So, I called. "Hey, Mom, I'm just letting you know that I'll be home in the morning."

"You get your ass home right now," she said.

"No, I won't be doing that. I'm calling to let you know that I'm safe, and that I'll be home in the morning."

"Traci, I'm not kidding. You come home, or you won't have a home to come home to."

"I'm sorry you feel that way, but I am not coming home until the morning." I hung up the phone, scared, but willing to take a stand. I was an adult and wanted to be treated like one.

The next morning, when I came home, my mom was sitting on the couch. "You need to move out. I'm not doing this with you anymore."

I'm not sure what she thought I would say, but I bet I surprised her when I said, "You're right."

In retrospect, she *was* right. It was her home, they were her rules (albeit, they were inconsistently applied), and there comes a time when two adult female family members should not be living under the same roof.

So I got a newspaper, called a company called Roommate Finders, and within a week had rented a room in an apartment right across the street from the beach. I was scared, but excited to move out on my own.

The night before I moved out, my mom knocked on my bedroom door. "You know, I was thinking, you don't have to go. You can stay. We just need to set some ground rules."

"No, you were right. It's time. I do need to go. I'm tired of fighting with you over every little thing. I'm sure you are too."

Her face changed from sad to angry. "Fine, Traci. Have it your way. You'll see that it's not as easy as you think it is out there in the real world. You've had it good here, and you'll see that soon enough. You'll be back. Mark my words."

The next morning, I packed the Mustang with my boxes, strapped my mattress on the roof, and started to pull out of the driveway. From the balcony above the driveway, I heard, "Wait! Wait!"

I looked up, and it was Chris. He went inside and came running out the front door. "You almost left without saying goodbye." We threw our arms around each other and hugged tightly, tears flowing. I'd never lived apart from him. We'd shared so many adventures and experiences that were just the two of us. He was fourteen, and we both knew that things would never be the same again.

"I love you, Christopher."

"Love you too, sis."

Later that night, as I lay on my mattress on the floor of an unfamiliar apartment, my first night living away from home, I could hear the waves of the Pacific Ocean crashing and the thick Scottish brogue of my roommates. I began to cry. I was alone and scared. But I vowed that night that I would prove my mother wrong. I would never ever go home again.

"Hey, Racy. How's the new place?" Richard asked. I called the next day to ask if I was still on their AAA policy.

"My car died, actually."

"Your car died? As in not fixable?"

I could hear my mom in the background. "That piece of shit car finally died?"

"Yeah, it's the axle. I want to sell it for parts and I wanted to know if I'm still on your AAA card so I can have it towed."

"Selling it for parts is a good idea. Yeah, you're still on the policy."

The next thing I know, my mom grabbed the phone and started yelling at me. "Oh you think you're just going to sell the car and keep the money? Don't forget that we gave you the Monte Carlo. We've been paying for your car insurance all this time. If you sell that car, I expect half the money."

"Are you serious? I literally just moved out and now don't have a way to get to work and you're going to take half the money? Nice, Mom. Really nice."

I hung up the phone and called AAA. Instead of selling the car for parts, I had my 1968 Mustang with the Mick Jagger bumper sticker towed to my parents' house, and I never saw it again.

A couple of days later, one of my roommates yelled my name from the other room. I literally couldn't understand a word he said, other than my name. "Tray-shee. Th' phane is fur ye."

"What?"

"Th' phane is fur ye." He was holding the telephone in the kitchen.

"Oh, the phone!" I took it, laughing. "Hello?" It was Richard.

"Hey, Racy. I'm just calling to see how things are going in your new apartment. Your roommates seem, uh, colorful."

"They are. I can't understand a word they say."

"So, listen. About your mom—"

I didn't say anything.

"She was pretty torn up about you leaving. Don't be too hard on her for how she acted. She loves you."

"She has a real funny way of showing it, Bear."

"Look. Mother and daughter relationships are always complicated. But you two will work it out. But if you ever need anything, just know you can come to me." His voice wavered a bit, and he said, "I'll always be here for ya, Racy. You're my baby girl."

Whether Linda Gordon and I would work it out would remain to be seen. But I didn't feel quite so scared to live on my own after that.

19.

You Just Know

Know When to Accept Things and Know When to Fight for What You Want

"Well, Racy. It looks like I'm moving to the land of woo-woos and hippies." The year was 1994 and Richard was moving to Sedona, Arizona, because my mother had moved there the year before.

The ten years since I'd moved out had gone quickly. My relationship with my mom had taken a major hit, and her disapproval of my life choices (as well as her reactions to them) caused a serious strain. I'd go home for holidays or when my mom had one of her various surgeries, but we really weren't all that close.

Thanksgivings at the Gordon house were unpredictable. Some years, it would be the quintessential Norman Rockwell experience, with the perfect turkey, Richard happily carving it, and everyone getting along. Other years, the champagne would flow a little too early in the day, Mom would forget about the turkey, burn it, serve dinner at 8:00 p.m., and pick embarrassingly personal fights at the table in front of all the guests. Some years, she just went on strike and boycotted it altogether. We never knew which kind of year it was going to be, until we were already there.

Richard just took it all in stride. "I love her, Racy. What am I gonna do?"

My mom and I eventually settled into a sort-of truce where she pretended that she accepted Ed, the man who became my first husband, my decision to move in with him before marriage, and the fact that we had our first child intentionally out of wedlock. For a woman who had been so wild in her youth, she was surprisingly disapproving of my unconventional choices. The older she got, the more conservative she became in her religious beliefs, in her politics, and in her personal life.

She came to my college graduation, my "surprise" wedding, and tried very hard to play the role of the loving mother.

All the time, Bear was just there. When you have as many kids as he had, you take their life choices in stride, apparently. He genuinely liked Ed, and was crazy about our baby, Madison. His easygoing nature was a wonderful buffer from the snide comments my mom would make.

They adopted a Malamute named Nika and kept one of her puppies and named him Apollo. Chris graduated from high school, Tom married Cathy and moved to San Diego, and life went on.

We'd drive down to San Diego for "astronaut events," like the twenty-fifth anniversary of Apollo 12. Being an astronaut's daughter was just something I did when there was an event or gathering. The rest of the time, I was going to college and graduate school, becoming a mother and wife, and focusing on my own life.

I didn't meet the crew of Apollo 11 very many times. Neil Armstrong and Buzz Aldrin were larger than life, and when we'd go to the astronaut events, if they were there, they were usually surrounded by hordes of people. Michael Collins was Richard's equivalent, "the guy who stayed on the ship," and was the most overlooked of the trio.

Imagine being "the guy who stayed on the ship" for the second trip to the moon! To this day, when I watch documentaries of the space program, more often than not, Richard isn't even mentioned. And yet, he never once complained. "That's just the way it is, Racy. You have to accept things the way they are. Not the way you want them to be."

"I'm moving to Arizona, Traci. Alone." She told me this during one of our rare moments of closeness. I can't say that I was surprised, as that was my mother's pattern. He was her fourth husband, after all. My mother left Richard in 1993 to move to Sedona, Arizona. She took Apollo and left him Nika.

I don't remember much about that time, other than how sad Bear seemed every time I saw him. He went to visit his kids, stayed busy at work, and lived in that big Manhattan Beach house all alone.

One day, I stopped by to see how he was doing and he had his old smile back. "You look good, Bear. Why? Didja get a new girlfriend or something?"

"Yeah!" He grinned. "She's a redhead, her name is Linda, and she lives in Sedona."

"What? How did this happen?" I was genuinely shocked.

"I flew out there and flat out told her, 'Look. You are my wife. I love you. Enough of this nonsense. You're not getting rid of me that easily, so I'm moving here to be with you. Wherever you go,

I am going to follow you, so you might as well just give it up now.'"

"Why?" I couldn't imagine why he would leave everything and follow her, after the way she'd treated him.

"I love her, Racy. What am I gonna do? So, it looks like I'm moving to the land of woo-woos and hippies." He looked so happy. "I got my Cookie back."

"What happened to 'You have to accept things the way they are. Not the way you want them to be?'" I still couldn't believe he was going.

Richard looked at me and grinned. "That's a real good question. I think it has to do with how likely it is you'll be able to change the outcome. In NASA, there wasn't much I could do about the decisions that came from above my head. Same thing with the military. You just have to accept it, because you're not gonna win that battle. But this thing with your mom, that's different. My marriage is worth fighting for. The outcome isn't set in stone, and I'll be damned if I'm gonna give up without a fight."

"How do you know the difference—which things to fight for and which things to let go of?" I was thinking of my own marriage now.

He shook his head wisely and said, "You just know."

20.

Life Goes On

You're Not Dead Yet

In many ways, Richard was a paradox. He was politically conservative, a family man, a Catholic who paid his bills on time and hated wasting money. He mowed his own lawn, made us do chores, and rarely ate out in restaurants.

But he was also a test pilot who broke the transcontinental speed record, an astronaut who endured thousands of hours of painful testing and preparation for space, and the hero who literally stepped out into space, wearing nothing but a suit made with 1969 technology. He was a Grand Marshal of the Rose Parade, dined with dignitaries and celebrities, and had a lifetime pass to the Rose Bowl. This from a guy whose favorite meal was

Stouffer's Creamed Chipped Beef, a frozen entrée more commonly known in the military as SOS (shit on a shingle).

The year was 1999. My first marriage had broken up, and I was remarried and seven months pregnant with my second child. My mom and Richard had apparently patched things up and seemed very happy. They'd moved (again) to Prescott, Arizona, and bought a beautiful home.

As time progressed, though, my relationship with my mom had drifted further apart. She'd gotten caught up in the role of astronaut wife (albeit thirty years too late) and took it upon herself to keep his legacy alive. I'm actually glad she did this, as there was a bunch of astronaut memorabilia that Bear had just stuck in boxes in the garage and moved from place to place. She took the trouble to categorize much of it. Things like flight records and personal notes had been just shoved in cardboard boxes and left forgotten. She did the world (and his family trust) a favor by going through it all and identifying items of value. My brother Chris and I often received boxes of "space stuff," which were the things not good enough for the Smithsonian, but still cool enough to keep.

The problem was, she also acted as Richard's gatekeeper—keeping him from the people and events that she deemed unsuitable. Unfortunately, I became one of the people she deemed unsuitable, and she made it very difficult for us to have a relationship. We would go years, only talking on his birthday, my birthday, and Father's Day. In fact, we developed a sort-of code so that we could talk without her listening. I'd call on his office fax line and hang up. He'd see the missed call, and when he could get away—say, to the dog park or the pharmacy—he'd call.

"How ya doin', Racy?"

"Happy Father's Day, Bear. Whatcha doin' today?"

"Oh, your mom is treating me real good. She ordered some lobster and we're having some brownies—my favorite. It's a good Father's Day."

"I'm glad she's treating you well, Bear. I miss you."

"I miss you too, BabyGirl. Maybe come and visit us sometime?"

"I will. Soon."

But we both knew that I couldn't.

"I'll call you on your birthday, okay?" My eyes filled with tears. This was so unfair.

"Sounds good, honey. I think I hear your mom coming. I gotta go. I love you."

"Love you too, Bear."

"Traci, turn on the news." My friend Kurt called to alert me to breaking news. "Third Man to Walk on Moon Dies in a Motorcycle Accident."

Oh my God. Pete. Bear's best friend. My first instinct was to pick up the phone and call him. But the years of distance with my mom caused me to hesitate. Would he want to hear from me? Would my mom let me talk to him?

I did the only thing I could think of. I called Chris. "Should I call him? I'm not sure."

Chris, being Chris, was blunt. "What would you want him to do if your best friend died?"

He was right, of course. So I made the call. Fortunately, Richard answered on the first ring.

"Hello?" His voice sounded husky.

"Bear? It's Racy. I just heard. I'm so—" I started to choke up. "I'm so very sorry."

His voice broke a little. "Thank you. I appreciate you calling."

"It was a motorcycle accident?"

"Yeah. I always told him that damn thing was gonna kill him someday. But, you know Pete."

"Yeah. What a terrible way to go."

He sighed and said, "Honestly, Racy, it's how he would have wanted to go. When we were in the Gemini 11 module, we had a lot of time to talk. He was prepared to die in service of space exploration. Hell, we all were. You don't take the kinds of risks we took and be afraid of death."

"That makes sense."

"Everybody dies. We all do. Some of us die in a blaze of glory and others die quietly in their room. No one gets out alive. I can't help but think that Pete would have wanted to go this way. I mean, he'll miss Nancy and the kids. But it's a helluva lot better than choking on a damn hot dog or something. You're not dead until you're dead. So you might as well die doing something you love, and don't act like you're dead until you are. Leave a legacy worth remembering. Know what I mean?"

"Yeah, I do."

"Dick? Who's on the phone?" I could hear my mother calling him from a distance.

"I gotta go, Racy. Thanks for calling. It means a lot."

"I'll call in October for your birthday."

"And bring that new baby around, when you get a chance. Life goes on."

"I will."

But we both knew I couldn't.

21.

The Last Supper

You Get to Decide What You'll Put Up with and What You Won't

"You should go, Traci." Pam wasn't often direct in her advice, but she seemed pretty clear about this. "You're always telling me how much you miss Richard, and now your mom has invited you to Thanksgiving."

"Right, but Pam, it's my *mom*. Those Thanksgivings. You know how brutal they can be."

"Right, but he hasn't even met Lea, and she's two years old. Just go. It's one day—two at most."

"I don't even know why she asked me to come. It has to be some kind of setup."

"Maybe. Or maybe what happened in New York got her thinking about family and how fast everything can change. Go. You might regret it if you don't."

It was November of 2001, and September 11th was still fresh in everyone's mind, and so I took her advice and I packed Lea into her car seat and made the 350-mile trek from Los Angeles to Prescott, Arizona. My husband was working the long weekend, and Madison always spent Thanksgivings with her dad's family.

"Who is this little angel?" Richard said as I brought Lea inside. I was instantly struck at how many mirrors, windows, and other reflective surfaces there were in the house. Someone likes looking at herself, I thought.

"My name is Lea but my daddy calls me AngelLea." Lea was tiny, with a bald head and deep voice, in a bright yellow dress. She stuck her hand out for a handshake, rather formally for a toddler.

Richard laughed and was instantly smitten. He reached out and enveloped her tiny hand with his big one. "Nice to meet you, Lea. I'm your Grandpa Bear."

I looked around the room and noticed we were alone. "Where's Mom?"

"Oh, she's resting. She should be out in a moment."

Resting? That seemed strange to me but before I could think too much about it, I heard Lea exclaim, "Mommy look!" She was looking at a distorted reflection of herself in a chrome trash can. "I look funny!" I grabbed my camera and snapped what would become one of my all-time favorite photos of her.

"Hey Racy." I heard my mom come into the kitchen. You don't get to call me that, I thought bitterly.

When I turned to look at her, I was confused. She looked like my mother, but she didn't. It was like one of those celebrity impersonators or a wax figure where everything is just slightly different. She'd apparently gotten veneers, even though she'd had perfect teeth. She was wearing some kind of wig that looked like her hair used to look. Even her voice sounded different. She was only fifty-six years old, so she wasn't elderly. She just did not look like herself to me.

"Hey, Mom." We embraced awkwardly, and then she turned her attention to Lea.

"Hey, Lea. Do you remember me? I'm your Grandma Linda. I haven't seen you since you were a baby." She went over to hug Lea, and Lea instinctively grabbed onto my leg.

Mom had come to see the baby a few months after she was born. The visit hadn't gone well, and resulted in another estrangement. "I don't know why I keep trying," I said to Pam, afterward. "Because that's what we do," she had answered.

The evening went as well as could be expected. Mom spent a lot of time in the kitchen making the family recipes that have now been passed down five generations. Chris was coming the next day, and it looked like it was going to be a Norman Rockwell Thanksgiving instead of one of the other ones.

"Racy, here. Stick this in your suitcase." Richard handed me some kind of receipt.

"What is this?" I asked as I took it.

"It's a Costco receipt."

"Why would I want one of your Costco receipts, Bear?"

"Look at the bottom. I signed it." He grabbed a yellow Post-it Note pad. "Here's another signature."

"What?" I was truly confused, as he started handing me random pieces of paper and signing them.

"It's my autograph. You can sell it, when the time comes. Get some money." He was smiling playfully.

"Bear. I'm not taking your Costco receipt and selling it. Don't be ridiculous." I put the items back on the table.

Little did I know that just a few years later eBay would be founded and I'd be able to see all kinds of his things on there. Kurt and I made a game of seeing who could find the strangest "Richard Gordon Astronaut" items on eBay. From old checks to the utility company from when he was married to Barbara to his white-turned-green lawn-mowing tennis shoes, it is a surreal experience to see your dad's personal effects being sold on eBay.

"Dick, can you pass the gravy?" My mom sat at one end of the dining table, Richard sat at the other, and the table was laden with my childhood memories. The same peacock patterned china that I'd spent hours hand washing as a teen sat next to the same Waterford crystal wine glasses that I used to sneak drinks from.

"What's the matter, Lea, don't you like Grandma's food?" My mom noticed that Lea wasn't eating much. "Did you let her eat too many Goldfish crackers before dinner, Traci?" She had that familiar look in her eyes, and what sounded like an innocent question most definitely was not. It was the beginnings of a fight.

My internal alarm system started to go off. Lea was sweet and innocent, and I did not want my mother's barbs to be directed at her. Fortunately, Bear saw it, too, and redirected the conversation.

"So, Chris. How's that job coming along?"

The conversation changed, but my protective sense had been activated. I was not going to be able to enjoy this dinner.

Rolls were passed, cranberry sauce was scooped, and the tone of my mother's voice continued to become sarcastic. It was just a matter of time before she picked a fight with one of us at the table. I was thirty-five years old and knew the routine all too well.

Chris was talking about his job and telling a story about some issue with his supervisor. Richard said to Chris, while looking directly at me, "Well, that's the thing about being an adult. You can decide what to put up with, and when to walk away."

It was then that my mom made some hostile comment designed to escalate conflict. I don't remember what she said or to whom she said it, but I do remember thinking, "Hey, wait. I am an adult. I don't have to do this with her anymore. I can walk away."

"Come on, Lea. Let's go change your diaper." I picked her up and we left the Thanksgiving dinner table, went to our room, and laid down. I was done.

For about twenty minutes, I laid there and listened to raised voices, and I was so happy to not be sitting at that table. I was free, and knew that I would never again sit at her Thanksgiving table.

"Do you think they fell asleep?" I heard my mom whispering from outside the door. "Should we wake them up for pie?"

"Just let them rest, Cookie. They can have pie in the morning."

I heard her voice fading away as she went in the direction of the kitchen. "That is just so weird. She just left in the middle of dinner."

I smiled and kissed Lea. Yes. I just walked away.

22.

Love Goggles

Beauty Is the Way It Makes You Feel

"I'll give you thirty minutes, Traci. We're busy and don't have a lot of time. And I don't want you coming to the house, so let's meet at Starbucks."

The year was now 2005 and Madison, Lea, and one-year-old David and I were visiting the Shoblom side of the family, who also happened to live in Prescott. I didn't really want to see my mom, but I did really want to see Bear and introduce him to my son.

"That's fine." *It'll be good to see you, too, Mom,* I thought, sarcastically.

It had been four years since I'd seen my mom, and she looked even weirder to me than before. She was wearing some kind of brace or shield over her rib cage, and when we stood next to each other, we were eye-to-eye. She'd always been four inches taller than I was, and even though old people shrink, this was something different.

"Hello, young man!" Bear swept David up off his feet and gave him, well, a bear hug. "I'm your Grandpa Bear."

"You were my Grandpa Bear first," Lea said, in her distinctively deep voice. "For four whole years."

"Hahaha, why yes I was. Whaddya say we go in and get you guys some chocolate milk?" He looked at me and said, "That okay, Racy?"

I nodded and they went inside, leaving me alone with my mom. "Are you okay?" I asked, looking at the brace.

"No, I'm not okay, actually." Her once clear blue eyes were yellowed and she had deep wrinkles that belied her age. She looked much older than sixty.

I felt a rush of empathy for her. "What's wrong?"

"Well, you know that I had my breast implants removed before we left California. They'd ruptured."

I nodded, as I'd helped her recuperate from that procedure.

"Apparently, all that silicone leaking into my system triggered an autoimmune disorder. All of the soft tissue in my body is, basically, being killed off by my immune system."

“Oh my God, Mom.” I wanted to hug her, but wasn’t sure how it would be received, so I didn’t.

“Anyway, I’m just doing the best that I can, but it’s not fun, I can tell you that.”

Before I could say anything else, Bear and the kids came out.

“Madison’s having coffee!” Lea said, trying to tattle on her big sister.

“She said you wouldn’t mind,” Bear said, grinning.

“I’m thirteen and my high school is literally across the street from a Starbucks,” Madison said. “I drink it all the time.”

Surreptitiously wiping tears from my eyes, I turned to them and said, “No problem, Bear. Thank you for getting them treats.”

“I’m getting tired, Bear. I’m gonna go wait in the car.” My mom started to limp toward the parking lot. “Have a safe trip home, Traci.”

“Can we go to our car?” Lea asked. “I wanna watch *SpongeBob*.”

“Yeah, it’s hot,” Madison said.

“Sure, take David.” I handed her the keys. “I won’t be long.”

“Those sure are some beautiful kids you got there, Racy,” he said, patting me on the back. “You done good.”

I turned to hug him. "Thanks, Bear." I pulled back and looked him in the eyes. "Mom looks—"

"Beautiful. Doesn't she?" That wasn't the word I was going to use, and he could tell. "She'll always be beautiful to me, because I love her. Beauty is the way someone makes you feel, not the way they look."

That was the way he looked at her throughout her whole illness, and it forever changed my mind about what beauty—and love—really is.

23.

SOS

Take Care of Yourself So That You Can Care for Others

I was standing in my kitchen when I got a call from Bear.

I'd been estranged, again, from my mom, for several years. It wasn't because of one big thing, but a series of little things. She'd tried to turn my daughters against me by buying them lavish gifts, and then ex-communicating them when it didn't work. She'd contacted my ex-husband and offered to help him get full custody of our daughter. Tried to drive a wedge in my marriage by contacting David Crisp, my childhood crush, and telling him that I still loved him, had named my son after him, and would leave my marriage if he came to California. (I did name my son after him, but with full consent of David's father. "What do I care about some crush you had when you were thirteen, Traci?") There were dozens of other, similar things.

At some point, I just said, "Enough is enough," and stopped writing or calling her.

Bear never called me, unless I had called him first, or it was my birthday. Needless to say, I was concerned when he called. "What's up, Bear?"

"Things are pretty rough with your mom, Racy. Really rough."

Now, this was a man who'd experienced breaking the sound barrier, had been through survival school, and had quit drinking and smoking with one decision. He'd been poked, prodded, and endured physical and emotional pain with zero complaint. "Pretty rough" had to be code for "really, really awful."

"What's going on?"

"I think her condition is affecting her thinking. She's, well, she's not acting right. I just thought you should know."

"Do you need me to come out?"

"I don't think so." His voice was choked with emotion. "I can handle it."

"Okay, let me know if you need me."

"Will do, Racy. I love you."

"Love you, too, Bear."

"I'm dying and I want to see you before I go." My mom left me a slurred voicemail late one night. "Please honor my request and come."

Well, what can I say to that? So I told my husband, Dan, what she'd said, and we agreed I should go. "I'll watch the kids, Traci. Just go."

So, I did. I drove 350 miles straight, crying, and singing loudly to John Mayer's *Say What You Need to Say,* stopping only to refuel. This was it. The final act of our forty-five-year drama.

When I arrived, I realized that Bear was correct. She wasn't acting right. This woman was not my mother. She was ravaged with disease and the prescription drugs she took to deal with the pain. She was barely recognizable as the woman she once was. In fact, she'd run into my father at the post office some months prior, and he didn't even recognize the mother of his children, except for her voice.

Bear, on the other hand, was coping as best he could. He'd pretty much stopped traveling, public speaking, or even visiting his kids so that he could take care of her. He had to feed her, bathe her, dress her, and take her to the doctor.

"I can't leave her. She needs me," he told us, when we suggested he get her some help.

"Look, Racy. I gotta show you somethin'." He brought me to the kitchen and opened the freezer. In it were, probably, twenty boxes of Stouffer's Creamed Chipped Beef. "I'm doin' okay. I'm taking care of myself so that I can take care of your mom."

While consuming vast quantities of SOS isn't quite what I'd consider a healthy diet, he was so proud of himself that I just hugged him and said, "I'm glad you're taking care of yourself, Bear."

"Well, she needs me around to take care of her. So that's what I'm gonna do."

And he did.

That night, I sat at her bedside and we talked. The room smelled funny from the oxygen and her nicotine patches, and there were fruit flies buzzing around half empty glasses of red wine. She looked small and frail and I realized that she no longer had the power to hurt me or anyone that I loved.

The next day, I got in my car and drove home to my children.

She was wrong about dying, then. It would be years before I heard from him again, except on my birthday. I didn't contact her because, in the words of John Mayer, I'd said what I needed to say.

24.
Well Played
Be the Bigger Person

The first serious loss I had in my life was not my mother, but my best friend Pam. She died, quite unexpectedly, while I was taking care of her after a post-breast-cancer reconstruction surgery that should have been very straightforward.

Pam's death absolutely devastated me. I think that grieving her as hard as I did gave me a new perspective on life. It was as Bear said when Pete died: You're not dead yet, and you have to leave a legacy worth remembering.

On my birthday, in 2017, a year after Pam had died, Bear called me. "Happy birthday, Racy. I was really sorry to hear about your friend Pam."

He knew a thing or two about losing friends, and his words comforted me, like a warm shower.

"Thank you, Bear. You sure know how it feels to lose someone you love."

Richard also said that my mom wanted to see me. She really was dying this time and wanted reconciliation. They'd moved (no surprise there) to San Marcos, California, and it was only a two-hour drive.

At first, I said no. I'd said everything I needed to say years before and didn't want any fake deathbed apologies. But then he said the fateful words that changed my mind.

"Please, Racy? As a favor to me?"

He had only asked me for a personal favor once before, in 1984. "Of course, I'll come," I said.

I emailed my mom and said, "I'd like to come see you, if that's possible. I'll bring the white flag."

She wrote back and said, "Of course it's possible to come and see me; it's an answered prayer."

"Okay, I'll come Saturday." I told my kids and my boyfriend Larry (my second marriage had broken up a few years before) that I was going to see my mom one more time.

"Good for you," they said. "You'll get some closure."

A few hours later, I got another email from her. The tone had completely changed. "May I ask what is the nature of the visit?"

The nature of the visit? She was the one who'd asked to see me!

"As you may know, Pam died last year. It really shifted my thinking about my decision not to see you. I'm thankful you're open to it." I was perplexed by the change in attitude. But, then again, not really.

"You are being vague," she replied. I didn't even get my reply composed when I got another email from her, five minutes later. "Traci, consider your invitation to visit rescinded."

That was the last conversation we ever had.

It was September 12, 2017. I was at my desk celebrating the fact that my first book, *The Power of Charisma*, had been published that day. I was excited for the book signings and events I planned to attend as part of marketing the book.

The phone rang, and I saw it was Bear. My heart sank.

"Hey, Racy," he said. I knew from the tone of his voice. "I have some bad news, I'm afraid. Your mom passed away last night. She went peacefully, thank God."

I couldn't even speak. I'd been wondering what it would feel like, but I didn't feel anything. "Okay. Am I invited to the funeral?"

"Of course you are, honey. I'll let you know when. I love you, Racy."

"Love you too, Bear."

She died on the day of my book launch. Well played, Linda Gordon. Well played.

25.

I Still Got It

Listen to Your Instincts

"I haven't seen him in five years," I said, as we were driving down the 405 freeway to Richard and my mom's San Marcos home. "I wonder if it will be weird?"

It had been a few days since my mom's death and her funeral was scheduled for the next day. I didn't want the first time I'd seen Bear in so long to be at a public gathering. My boyfriend Larry and I had been dating for six years, but he'd never met either my mother or Richard.

Chris had suggested that maybe this wasn't the time to make the introduction, and Larry graciously agreed. But he knew I was grieving and too upset to drive, so he drove me and kindly waited outside while I went in to see my dad for the first time since his wife had died.

"Hey, Racy," he said, from the couch. "Sorry I can't get up for a hug right now."

I went over and kissed the top of his head and sat down next to him. "No worries at all, Bear." He turned to embrace me and I said, "You look good!"

He did! He looked tired, of course. His wife had just died and he'd spent the last ten years as her caregiver. But his hazel eyes were still clear and alert, and he looked basically the same as he always had.

"I still got my hair," he said proudly. "And it's still brown." He patted his head. "Mostly, haha. Not bad for eighty-seven, right? I still got it."

I laughed and said, "You do." I reached out to stroke his head. His hair had always been so soft and fine, and it still was. "It's really good to see you."

"You too. You're my baby girl." His voice caught. "You were always welcome here, you know that, right?"

I wasn't, but I said, "Yeah. But, you know how things were."

"Yeah. I'm sorry for that."

"Me too."

A moment passed, and he said, "How do you like the new place? I got it for your mom and pretty much set it up all by myself. Well, Tom and his friend Joe helped me, of course."

Cathy had told me they moved to San Marcos and that her ex, my brother Tom, was going to live with Bear so that they could kind of take care of each other. I was surprised at how familiar the place felt, considering I'd never been there.

"Let me give you a tour." Richard got up and wobbled a little as he navigated around the couch.

"Be careful, Dad," I heard Tom say from his room.

"Tom has been really good to me," he said.

I got a quick tour of the place and had a moment alone in the room where my mother had died. I wanted to feel her presence and get the closure I didn't get when she was alive.

When I went back out to the living room, Bear was back on the couch, watching football. I was aware of Larry waiting outside and didn't want to stay for long. Everyone was preparing for the funeral the next day.

"You feeling okay?" I asked.

"I'm okay." He turned to look at me. "They think I had a stroke. I fell and hit my leg. But I'm not so sure."

"Well, what do you think? Do you think it was a stroke, or just that you lost your balance?"

"I don't know. Probably if I had to guess, I'd say no. But I am aware that my thinking is a little fuzzy and my speech is a little slow. But my wife just died, so it could be that. I just don't know."

"Listen. If there's one thing I know about you, it's that you are objective about your body. It was, literally, government property at one point. You were a NASA pincushion for years and know more about your own body and how it works than pretty much anyone else. So listen to your instincts about what you think is going on."

I stood up to kiss him on the cheek. "But for now, you rest. Tomorrow is going to be a difficult day. We can deal with the other stuff later."

"Okay, Racy. I love you. See you tomorrow."

26.

Maybe Enough's Enough

Don't Be Afraid of Dying

Despite the fact that my mom had converted to Catholicism some years prior, her celebration of life was held in their home.

Honestly, my memories of the day are a bit hazy, as is to be expected. Larry and my daughter Lea came to support me. Chris and his wife, Liz, hosted the event, and our brother Larry Gordon flew in. My mom's sisters were there, too, and I hadn't seen them in decades.

I was particularly happy that many of Richard's astronaut-era friends were there. Michael Collins came to support him, as well as a lot of the familiar faces from those crazy days with Pete.

It was a warm tribute, and we lit candles and floated them in a small fountain in honor of her.

There were Bible passages read, and my mom's paintings were displayed, proudly. I had no idea she'd become such a talented artist.

After the service, I saw Bear sitting in a chair next to the dining table, looking pale. "How ya doin', Bear? Can I get you a sandwich or something?" Liz and my mom's sisters were in the kitchen starting to put out food.

"Maybe later. I'm not feeling so good."

"Maybe go lie down for a spell? No one would blame you a bit."

"That might be a good idea."

A few minutes later, Chris called me aside. Larry Gordon was standing at the end of the hallway, outside the master bedroom. "We have a situation," Chris said, in low tones. "Bear isn't feeling well, and the paramedics are on the way. We're going to need to clear some space for the stretcher."

My head started to spin. What? Paramedics? Stretcher? This was a funeral!

Chris followed me back out to the living room and took complete command of the situation. "We're going to need everyone to relocate to the exterior portion of the residence," he said.

"What he means is that we need everyone to go out on the patio," Liz said, following him.

Looking back on it, I am impressed and grateful to Chris that he handled everything the way he did. This was his mother's funeral too. And our dad was literally carried out of it on a stretcher.

The guests—family and friends—stood aside, and Chris and Larry Gordon followed the ambulance to the hospital.

After they left, I went into the kitchen where Liz was standing, and we looked around. There were probably thirty people standing in the living room, stunned speechless. "What do we do now?" I asked.

Liz gave me a hug and whispered in my ear. "Alcohol. Time to break out the wine and food."

Bear was in the hospital for a few days while they ran some tests to find out what was wrong. He was right. It hadn't been a stroke. He had cancer. All those years taking care of his wife had taken a toll, and he'd ignored his own health in service of making sure my mom had the care she needed.

He came home to recuperate, and Larry and I made the two-hour drive down several times. It was so wonderful to be able to see him again, and I loved bringing him and Tom home-cooked food.

"Hey, Bear, happy birthday," I said in early October, calling the house phone. No more secret calls were needed. "Sorry, I can't come down. I'm working and the kids have a thing at school."

"No problem, honey. Al flew in and we're having a little birthday party. I'll save you a piece of cake."

That weekend, Larry and I drove down for a visit. "How was your party, Bear?"

"It was good! Real good to see Al." A shadow crossed his eyes and his prominent brow furrowed.

"What?" I asked.

He sighed. "I don't know, Racy. Al and I got to talking, and I told him—I'm starting to wonder, maybe enough's enough."

"What do you mean?"

"I mean, I'm eighty-eight years old. I've done things in my life that few men ever get to do. What else is left? I've had a good run of it. Maybe I'm done."

I paused a minute and asked, "Are you scared to die?"

He grinned and started laughing. "Hell, no. I have my faith. And I've got my Cookie and Jimmy on the other side waiting for me."

Tears stung my eyes. I couldn't imagine what it would feel like to have that kind of courage and faith. "Well, Bear, I hope you stick around for a long time. We still need you."

Richard shook his head, as if to shake off the dark thoughts and said, "How 'bout you bring me some of that birthday cake?"

"You got it, Bear."

27.

The Final Countdown

Sometimes You Don't Get the Chance

In the eight weeks after my mom died, we got into a pattern. I'd make home-cooked meals, and Larry and I would drive down to San Marcos for a visit. Sometimes Lea would come. My nephews were there once. We'd watch football and just talk.

Some of the conversations were deep. "I don't understand why you did it, Bear. Why did you stay with my mom when she treated you so badly?"

"She was the love of my life. I made a commitment to her and I wanted to honor it."

Some of the conversations were funny. I gave him a signed copy of *The Power of Charisma*, and he said, "You wrote a book, Racy? Were they able to read your handwriting?"

Other conversations reflected his past adventures. When Larry shared a story with him about taking his Porsche 911 Carrera across the desert at 185 miles an hour, Richard just grinned and asked him, "Why'd you stop?"

I was so glad to finally get a chance to know him again. He was still the brilliant, witty, courageous, loyal man that I'd known since I was twelve years old.

"All right, Bear. We need to be heading back," I said one evening in November. "What do you want me to bring for next time?" I was already thinking about Thanksgiving and how different it would be from the ones prior.

"Brownies. Definitely bring some more brownies. See ya, Racy. I love you."

"Love you, too, Bear."

Sadly, I never got the chance to bring him those brownies. I got the call from Chris early one morning, a few days later. "Hey, sis. I have bad news." Richard had passed away from cardiac arrest and complications of cancer, eight weeks and one day after my mom had passed away.

He literally died of a broken heart and kept his promise to my mom when he moved to Sedona: "Wherever you go, I will follow you."

Richard had two memorial services. The first one was in Washington state, where his surviving siblings lived. I didn't go to that one, because it was the family from his "Barbara-era." It didn't feel like it was my place to go. Cathy told me that it was a warm, loving event and many of Richard's extended family had attended. That must have been a big crowd!

I recall seeing a photo of Richard at Barbara's funeral a few years back. He had so many family members in that photo that they practically needed a drone to capture everyone. He had five surviving biological children, and they were Catholic. So each of my stepsiblings have numerous children, and those children were adults and having kids of their own. Richard took the "go forth and multiply" directive very literally. He was the definition of a family man and loved babies more than just about anyone I know.

The second service was to be at Arlington National Cemetery. It takes some time to plan an event like that, and although he'd passed away in November, that service wouldn't be until the following February.

January of 2018, Larry and I had gone to Ferndale, California, to visit my father, and I was sitting in the backseat of my stepmom Lynne's car on our way to dinner when my cell phone rang. It was Larry Gordon.

"Hey, Larry."

He sounded uncomfortable. "Hey, Traci. So, as the executor of the Gordon Family Trust, I wanted to give you a heads-up about some documents you'll be receiving in the mail next week."

"Okay?"

"Yeah, so, you aren't included in the trust."

"I was written out of the will?" I felt like I'd been sucker-punched.

"Yeah. Your mom included someone else. Who's Terry?"

"She's my sister."

"Oh! I didn't know your mom had another daughter." Larry sounded confused.

"She didn't. That's my father's daughter."

"I see. Anyway, I hate to be the bearer of bad news. I just didn't want you to be surprised when you get the documents next week. I'm sorry, Traci."

Tears filled my eyes. "Thanks, Larry."

Cognitively it made sense. Terry had been much closer to my mom than I was. The Gordon Family Trust was my mom's estate, too, and she chose to give my share to Terry. I wasn't mad at my sister, or even my mom.

It just hurt. My siblings would go on to inherit the astronaut stuff of value from the trust. My mother left me her leavings. I inherited her dish towels and furniture. "No, thank you," I said, when they asked if I wanted anything from the San Marcos home. "I don't want anything from her."

The whole thing was terribly embarrassing. My siblings were left to wonder, "What did Traci do that was so bad to get her written out of the will?" I had no answer for that, sadly.

I even started to second-guess my relationship with Richard. Had he really loved me? Did I imagine the whole thing? It was a very dark time in my life, grieving two parents who'd died within weeks of each other, and wondering where I fit in the family circle.

Years later, when I finally had the courage to read the documents I'd been sent, I saw that Bear tried to write me back into the will. His shaky handwriting was in the margins of the pages, with my name and a question mark. But he died before he ever got the chance.

28.

The Right Stuff

The Ordinary Is What's Extraordinary

"We're running a bit late, but we'll be there soon." I called Larry Gordon's wife, Nancy, the night before the funeral to let her know we were on our way to her home for the private family wake.

"No rush, we're all here," she said, in her gentle Southern voice. "It'll be good to see you."

Funerals are often the only family reunions some families experience. That was certainly the case with us. I don't recall any other event where all of Richard's surviving kids, their spouses, and most of his grandchildren were present.

I was really nervous as we pulled our rental car into the driveway of Larry and Nancy's home. I wasn't sure how I would be received after the stunt my mom pulled with the family trust. I hadn't seen Chris since our mom's funeral. Would it be strange? Would they look at me as the black sheep of the family? Was I even really family?

"It's go time," I said to David, Lea, and Larry, as we got out of the car.

"You got this, Mom," Lea said.

"We gotchu," David answered, opening the back door of the car.

Larry grabbed my hand and we rang the bell. "It's open!" someone said from the inside.

The minute I walked in the door, I had my answer. "Traci!" Nancy came right up and hugged me. There was kindness and warmth in her eyes. "The food's in there, drinks are over there. I think your brother is, oh, somewhere. Make yourself at home."

Everyone was there. Carleen, Rick, Larry, Tom, Diane, and Chris. Even though I never met Jimmy, I could swear I felt his presence too. The home was filled with Richard's kids, their spouses, and many grandchildren and friends.

At one point, I found myself in the kitchen, talking to the sisters. Carleen, Diane, Nancy, and I stood there and reminisced. We commented on how different our experiences had been growing up with Richard. He was the same man, with the same values his whole life, but environment really does shape our experiences with a person. Every single one of his kids had a different relationship with Richard than the others.

"See you in the morning," we said, as we walked back to the rental car. The public service at Arlington National Cemetery was going to be a once-in-a-lifetime experience. But that family gathering had filled in some of the cracks in my heart.

"Arrived." Our GPS announced that we'd made it to Arlington, but we really didn't need her to tell us that. Arlington National Cemetery is one of our country's most beautiful places. Towering trees, neatly kept grounds, sweeping gates, and colorful flowers tell visitors that this is the final resting place of many of our country's most significant figures.

"Is this where the presidents are buried?" Lea asked, as we walked across the parking lot.

"No, actually only two presidents are buried here. John F. Kennedy is one of them. Most of them are buried at home," I answered.

"You mean they could have put Grandpa Bear on the golf course?" David cracked, referring to Richard's San Marcos home overlooking a golf course.

"Did you know that the first grave was put here in 1864?" Lea said, looking at her phone.

"Isn't that the year you were born, Mom?" David has always been a master of breaking tension with humor. "Seriously, though, how come Grandpa Bear is being buried here?"

"Because of his military background," Larry said. "You're not likely to ever see a more formal funeral again in your lifetimes."

The mood shifted as we walked in the building. My siblings and their families were all gathered in a waiting room, along with friends, dignitaries, and others. The only one I really recognized was Al Bean.

It struck me that it had to be really odd for Al. Pete had been buried here in 1999, and now Richard was being interred. It was a complete preview of his own funeral, with only the family members different.

The day was warm and bright, but our hearts were heavy as we followed the caisson down the path to the gravesite. A rolling sea of black-clad mourners walked surprisingly quickly, following the horse-drawn casket. As expected, an American flag was draped over it.

Dozens of men and women stood in full uniform, saluting as the pallbearers carried the casket to the gravesite. The military band added to the momentous feeling, and I couldn't help but think of all the other heroes whose families had had the same exact experience. We were now part of history, part of the tapestry that weaves through the United States of America.

I don't remember much of what was said at the service. The backdrop of "Taps," played on bagpipes to honor Richard's Scottish heritage served as a soundtrack as my lifetime of memories as his daughter flooded my mind. Meeting him on the plane. Watching him dance with my mom in the kitchen while doing dishes. Him explaining to me the rules of football. Telling me he was proud of me, and calling me his baby girl.

The twenty-one-gun salute was somber, and when they folded the flag and handed it to Carleen, his eldest child, there was not a dry eye to be found.

Shortly before the service ended, it was time for the flyover. We stood silently, necks craned toward the clear blue sky, for several minutes. I heard them before I saw them. A cluster of jets flew over our heads.

One plane broke formation and veered away from the others. It was Richard, silently going "Woo hooo!" as he flew off into eternity. Now you can see what's out there, Bear. Beyond the moon.

After the service, the crowd began to disperse. "Are we going, Mom?"

"Just a minute. I have something I need to say to Bear."

Richard's grandkids crowded around his casket, having their own moment of goodbye. I waited until everyone had gone, and then Larry and I walked over to Richard's grave. He stood respectfully back, and I approached the shiny wooden casket and laid my head on one end and wept.

"Hey, Bear. I'm not sure if I'm talking to your head or your feet." I chuckled through my tears. "I sure hope it's your head.

"I'm sorry I never got to bring you those brownies. But I want to thank you. Thank you for your patience with me. For being the calming place in my relationship with my mom. Thank you for being the one person she didn't drive away. Mostly, though, Bear, thank you for being my dad. We had quite an adventure, you and me. I will keep your legacy alive. I promise you that, sir."

As I stood up to join the rest of my family, the vista of endless white headstones imprinted in my mind. Every one of them represented a person. Yes, they were national heroes. But to someone, they were an ordinary mom or dad, brother or sister, son or daughter. Even the most extraordinary accomplishments are made by ordinary people.

Richard Gordon was a simple man with solid values and a profound work ethic. He took risks to achieve his dreams, and sometimes they paid off. He handled disappointments with grace and kept his sense of playfulness and wonder throughout his life.

Most of us won't become space explorers. But every single one of us has the potential to become great.

In the end, I didn't get the astronaut stuff from my relationship with Richard. I got something infinitely more valuable. I got the Right Stuff.

Lessons I Learned from My Astronaut Dad

- ★ Don't compare yourself to anyone else
- ★ Do it right the first time
- ★ Give it your all
- ★ We're just humans floating on a rock in space
- ★ Not every problem is serious
- ★ Happy wife, happy life
- ★ Keep secrets
- ★ A good friend lasts a lifetime
- ★ Everyone fails
- ★ Don't go along with things that you know are wrong
- ★ Never leave someone in peril
- ★ There's a difference between irreverence and disrespect
- ★ Handle disappointment graciously
- ★ Trust is everything

★ Sacrifice for a greater goal
★ If you're going to lie, make sure you get away with it
★ You can't rebel against authority when you make the choice
★ Know when it's time to go
★ Know when to accept things and when to fight for what you want
★ You're not dead yet
★ You get to decide what you'll put up with and what you won't
★ Beauty is the way it makes you feel
★ Take care of yourself so that you can care for others
★ Be the bigger person
★ Listen to your instincts
★ Don't be afraid of dying
★ Sometimes you don't get the chance
★ The ordinary is what's extraordinary

"There's nothing between you and oblivion except a pressure suit, and you just can't afford to get out there and get in a big rush and tangle yourself up where nobody can help you. . . . The biggest thing I've learned from the people that have gone in the past, you simply have to take your time, and you can't exhaust yourself."

—Richard F. Gordon Jr.
Apollo 12

Acknowledgments

Special thank you to my "sisterfriend" Cathy Gordon for helping me remember details, dates, and the order of events. And for bearing witness to those crazy Thanksgivings!

Also, thank you to my "radio dad" Lee Shoblom, for being my father and my role model for how to thrive in a blended family.

About the Author

Traci Shoblom is one of eight children raised by Apollo astronaut Richard F. Gordon Jr.

Her book *The Power of Charisma: Using the C-Factor to Inspire Change* (coauthored with the former Vice President of Nightingale Conant Dan Strutzel) hit the shelves in 2017. It was followed by *The Power of Positive Selling*, *The Growth Mindset*, and the yet-to-be-released *WIN*.

Traci created five fully produced Nightingale Conant audio programs (including the best-selling *The Top 2%*), as well as five books of her own, including *ACE Your Decisions: ACES and the Angry Employee* (with Dr. Larry Pate); *Motherhood, Apple Pie, and Other Fattening Things*; *How to Become a Life Coach*; *If I Die Before I Wake* (with June Sharman); and *How NOT to Write a Book*. She has also penned several unauthored vegetarian cookbooks and has authored dozens of articles, whitepapers, and academic chapters and cases. In addition, Traci has written hundreds of video scripts, audio scripts, and radio-television advertisements.

In the nearly twenty-five years since she earned her master's degree in psychology, Traci has ghost-written for and worked with leaders, celebrities, and organizations in almost every field, including Dale Carnegie Training, Ken Blanchard, Anthony Robbins, Les Brown, Brian Tracy, Marshall Goldsmith, Dr. Mark Hyman, David Bach, T. Harv Eker, Jim Fannin, Nightingale Conant, and Herbalife, among others.

A popular speaker, Traci has also been featured at Story Expo, the conference for Hollywood screenwriters.

A passionate vegan and an award-winning photographer, Traci lives in a stone cottage in Glendora, California, with three huge dogs and three annoyed cats. Her three adult children are each off pursuing their own dreams.

About Richard F. Gordon Jr.

Richard Francis Gordon Jr. (October 5, 1929–November 6, 2017) was an American naval officer and aviator, chemist, test pilot, and NASA astronaut, and an American football executive. He was one of twenty-four people to have flown to the moon, as the Command Module Pilot of the 1969 Apollo 12 mission, which orbited the moon forty-five times. Prior to his lunar flight Gordon had flown in space as the pilot of the 1966 Gemini 11 mission.

He won the Bendix Trophy race from flying between Los Angeles to New York City in May 1961, in which he established a new speed record of 869.74 miles per hour and a transcontinental speed record of two hours and forty-seven minutes.

He logged more than 4,500 hours flying time with 3,500 hours of those hours in jet aircraft. He was also a student at the Naval Postgraduate School at Monterey, California. Gordon logged a total of 315 hours and 53 minutes in space, of which 2 hours and 41 minutes were spent in space walks outside the vehicle.

After Apollo 12, Gordon was assigned as backup Commander of Apollo 15. He was slated to walk on the moon as Commander of Apollo 18, but that mission was canceled because of budget cuts.

After his flights, Gordon worked in the astronaut office. He became the Chief of Advanced programs in 1971. Gordon worked on the design of the Space Shuttle.

After leaving NASA, Gordon served as Executive Vice President of the New Orleans Saints Professional Football Club in the National Football League (1972–1976); was General Manager of Energy Developers, Limited (EDL), a Texas partnership involved in a joint venture with Rocket Research Corporation for the development of a liquid chemical explosive for use in the oil and gas industry (1977); President of Resolution Engineering and Development Company (REDCO), which provided design and operational requirements for wild oil well control and firefighting equipment onboard large semi submersible utility vessels (1978); following the REDCO merger with Amarco Resources, Gordon assumed the additional duties of Vice President of Marketing, Westdale, an oil well servicing subsidiary of AMARCO operating in North Central Texas and Oklahoma, and also served as Vice President for Operations, Texas Division (1980); served as Director, Scott Science and Technology, Inc., Los Angeles Division (1981–1983).

In March 1982 he became President of Astro Sciences Corporation. This company provided a range of services including engineering, project management, project field support teams, to software and hardware system design for control room applications. In the summer of 1984, Gordon was a Technical Advisor for and played the part of "Capcom" in the CBS miniseries *Space* by James A. Michener.

Gordon served as Chairman and co-Chairman of the Louisiana Heart Fund, Chairman of the March of Dimes (Mother's March), Honorary Chairman for Muscular Dystrophy, and on the boards of directors for the Boy Scouts of America and Boys' Club of Greater New Orleans.

Richard was married twice, to Barbara Field and Linda Saunders. From his first marriage, he raised six children: Carleen, Richard, Lawrence, Thomas, James, and Diane. From his second marriage, he raised two stepchildren: Traci and Christopher.

Awards and Honors Received

★ Navy Astronaut Wings
★ NASA Distinguished Service Medal
★ NASA Exceptional Service Medal
★ Bendix Trophy in 1961
★ Two Navy Distinguished Flying Crosses
★ Navy Distinguished Service Medal
★ Phi Sigma Kappa Merit Award in 1966
★ Institute of Navigation Award for 1969
★ Godfrey L. Cabot Award in 1970
★ Rear Admiral William S. Parsons Award for Scientific and Technical Progress in 1970
★ Manned Spacecraft Center (MSC) Superior Achievement Award
★ NASA Group Achievement Award
★ Richard Gordon Elementary School in Kingston, Washington, named after him

★ Inducted into the International Space Hall of Fame with nine of his Gemini astronaut colleagues in 1982

★ Inducted into the United States Astronaut Hall of Fame on March 19, 1993

★ Grand Marshal, Rose Parade 1970

CPSIA information can be obtained
at www.ICGtesting.com
Printed in the USA
JSHW031922170123
36222JS00004B/4

9 781722 506407